T0293924

WHEN THE
SKY WAS BLUE

RICH CHAMBERLAIN

WHEN THE
SKY WAS BLUE
The Inside Story of
Coventry City's Premier League Years

First published by Pitch Publishing, 2023

Pitch Publishing
9 Donnington Park,
85 Birdham Road,
Chichester,
West Sussex,
PO20 7AJ
www.pitchpublishing.co.uk
info@pitchpublishing.co.uk

ISBN 978 1 80150 462 1

Typesetting and origination by Pitch Publishing
Printed and bound in India by Thomson Press

Contents

Contents

Acknowledgements

THERE ARE many people without whom this book wouldn't exist. First and foremost, I must thank Suzanne, Isaac and Elijah. Thank you for living through the putting together of this book with me and never grumbling when I uttered the words, 'I've just got an interview to do tonight.' Boys, I hope that being a Coventry fan fills your childhoods with as much joy as it did mine.

To my parents, John and Maggie, and brother Gaz for your huge role in my path as a Coventry fan. For introducing me to the often-demoralising life of following this club, taking me to matches and ensuring I had everything from the latest kit to the club wallpaper.

I've been incredibly fortunate to be given so much help in putting this book together. The following all gave their time to be interviewed and did so free of charge. I didn't want this to be a book of my memories, I wanted it to be the story of Coventry's Premier League years through the memories of the players, managers and key individuals who were there. I was bowled over by the amount of time given up by many of my childhood heroes – my inner teenage self was dying of happiness throughout these conversations. This book couldn't exist without the input of these interviewees. A huge thank you to:

Bobby Gould, Ron Atkinson, Gordon Strachan, Steve Ogrizovic, Stewart Robson, Trevor Peake, Micky Gynn, Micky Quinn, Peter Ndlovu, Jonathan Gould, Tony Sheridan, Willie Boland, Gavin Strachan, Dion Dublin, Cobi Jones, Brian Borrows, Nigel Winterburn, Roy Wegerle, John Williams, Robert Rosario, Dave Busst, David Burrows, Julian Darby, Peter Atherton, Liam Daish, John Salako, Richard Shaw, Marcus Hall, Darren Huckerby, Noel Whelan, Magnus Hedman,

7

Trond Egil Soltvedt, Laurent Delorge, Simon Haworth, John Aloisi, John Eustace, Youssef Chippo, David Thompson, Steve Froggatt, Barry Quinn, Cédric Roussel, Robbie Keane, Carlton Palmer, John Hartson, Bryan Richardson, Rob Gurney, Stuart Linnell, Andy Turner, Graham Hover, Ray Clarke, Jim Brown and Martin Bodenham.

Many of the interviewees were traced through social media but I also had assistance from a selection of incredible helpers in tracking down former players. Thank you to Ed Blackaby, Neil Littlewood, Mark Hornby, Amie Mole, Pete Oliver and James Penny. Support was also readily available from Russ Crow, Rich Williams, Justin Heath, Adi Iliff, Robert Siney (the fantastic @PremiershipYrs on Twitter), Ryan Woodward, Kevin Ward, Jazz Lyons and Libby Luscombe. A big thanks for having faith in my writing must be given to Pat Ross, Chris Barnes, Tor Clark and Rob Laing.

I'm fortunate to have benefited from the excellent writing and reporting of many authors and broadcasters who have covered Coventry and '90s football. Thank you to Steve Phelps, Andy Turner, Rob Gurney, Simon Gilbert, Jim Brown, Jim Keoghan, Tom Flight, Rick Gekoski, James Adams, Adam Sloman, Jonathan Strange and Paul Gilbert. The array of Coventry-related social media accounts have also been invaluable, including Sky Blues Fan TV, Deano's Sky Blue Memories, Sky Blues Extra and the Sky Blue View. An extra thank you to Mr View Sky for his incredible collection of '90s highlights and goal videos that made reliving these memories even more of a joy. A special thank you to everyone at Pitch Publishing, particularly Jane, Ivan, Graham, Dean and Duncan, for making the dream of this book a reality.

Thank you to everyone who has supported this book, from friends and family to those who have commented, liked and shared social media posts. I can't thank you all enough for your support. I hope you enjoy the journey through Coventry's Premier League years.

Introduction

The Beginning

COVENTRY CITY'S Premier League era began on 15 August 1992 with a home fixture against Middlesbrough. But, to get a real understanding of where the Sky Blues were as they entered this brave new dawn, it might be wise to rewind a few years before we get there. This will just be a whistle-stop tour to lead us into the Premier League years, but I feel it's a merited detour. So, where to start?

Oh, go on then, let's briefly head back to the 1987 FA Cup Final, a match I must admit to having precisely zero recollection of as I was just a year old at the time. Still, we all know that Coventry lifted the famed piece of silverware that day, prompting co-manager John Sillett to proclaim shortly afterwards that the club would be shopping 'in Harrods rather than Woolworths' from there on in. The future promised so much and a tenth-placed finish the following year wasn't a bad return at all.

The next season was even better, as the mouth-watering attacking prowess of Cyrille Regis and David Speedie helped the club to seventh. The good times, unfortunately, couldn't last. An FA Cup humbling against minnows Sutton United in that 88/89 season gave a glimpse of what was to come. The 1989/90 campaign saw a slide to 12th in the final league table. This was far from a disaster, but still represented a significant drop from the previous year. Nevertheless, it was still a huge surprise when, in November 1990, John Sillett was sacked.

'It was a big shock,' says club stalwart Trevor Peake, who had been at the heart of the City defence for seven years at the time of Sillett's sacking. 'It didn't make a lot of sense to us. We weren't where we wanted to be and we could have probably played better and had more wins to help John keep his job but we were very surprised when the news came.'

'We were so shocked,' adds FA Cup-winning midfielder Micky Gynn. 'We'd had three very good seasons. We weren't even really struggling when he was sacked. He was in bed poorly at the time and to be sacked like that was a disgrace. If Coventry achieved what he achieved now, you would take that all day long.'

What made the dismissal all the more surprising was the fact that Sillett had discussed moving some of his senior players into coaching roles, putting them on the path to management. What had looked like a long-term succession plan – Coventry's version of Liverpool's boot room, perhaps – was now up in smoke.

'Me and Cyrille had been called into the office and John's plan was to prepare us for coaching and management,' Peake adds. 'Myself and Cyrille spent a bit of time in John's room talking about the future and what he was imagining the future might be. He said he wanted us to be part of it.'

One man who has seen it all down the years when it comes to Coventry City is broadcaster Stuart Linnell. He too admits great surprise at the sacking of the man who he, and many others, affectionately refers to as Snoz.

'I got on very well with Snoz and I got on very well with the chairman at the time, John Poynton,' says Linnell. 'I don't know if John would admit it now but I think he was hasty in his decision to get rid of Snoz. Snoz never really reconciled himself or forgave John for that, he felt he had been unfairly treated. One or two things weren't quite right maybe but he had done a great job with us. Things didn't go well after Snoz's sacking.'

That's putting it lightly. If sacking the much-loved 'Snoz' was a shock, his replacement was a gobsmacking choice. In came England's Italia 90 hero Terry Butcher, who stepped into his first managerial role. Controversially, he came in as player-manager, with two contracts: one as a player and the other as a manager.

'What the club did, in retrospect, was mad,' says club historian Jim Brown. 'Signing Butcher and giving him a playing contract and a managing contract was mad. The chairman had the club's interests at heart and thought it was the right decision. It was the wrong decision, unfortunately.'

On paper, it was undoubtedly an exciting appointment. Butcher had captained England to the semi-final of the World Cup just a few months earlier and here he was rocking up at Highfield Road. However, this wasn't the Terry Butcher of Italia 90.

'He came in as a player-manager but his knee was knackered,' Gynn recalls. 'I'm not sure how he passed a medical. He rarely played and rarely trained. Terry shouldn't have been there in the first place, John should have been the manager. All of this was done with no involvement from the players, which I also found astonishing. Every single one of the lads was disappointed for John to be sacked. It was always going to be a difficult job for Terry. Our feelings went out of the window when we stepped on to the pitch and you always give your all. It did spoil an era for Coventry City, though, that could have gone on for a lot more years.'

Butcher managed just six appearances at the heart of the Coventry defence due to injury. While a lack of time on the pitch may have given him more opportunity to focus on his managerial role, there were more than a few who called into question some of his decisions. In fact, many were puzzled at Butcher's treatment of some of the older heads in the dressing room. The writing was seemingly on the wall for many of the club's FA Cup heroes.

'What a great player Terry was,' says Peake. 'He had an injury, meaning his appearances were limited. He was looking to sign a couple of centre-halves, so I could see that I wasn't part of his plans. That's fair enough, I was 34 years old. Before John was sacked, I didn't have any thoughts of anything other than ending my career at Coventry.'

Butcher had other ideas, and during a controversial pre-season trip to Scotland, Peake was one of three players (alongside Kenny Sansom and Lloyd McGrath) to be sent home. The iconic defender was stripped of the captaincy and soon shipped out to Luton. He wasn't the only one to be shown the exit.

'He basically told Regis that he wasn't wanted,' Jim Brown adds. 'That was a strange decision and fans were concerned. He got rid of David Speedie way before his time as well. Kilcline went too. Butcher didn't want the old guard, that was absolutely clear. The first season was okay, the home form was good but people realised by Christmas of the 1991/92 season that we were in for a real struggle. There was a Friday night game where we lost against Luton 1-0 and we were absolutely shocking. The writing was on the wall for Butcher.'

One of the old guard who was kept on was full-back Brian Borrows. Looking back on Butcher's reign all these years on, Bugsy is another name in the column of those for whom Butcher tried to change too much too soon.

'It was Terry's first managerial job and there was a lot of experience in that team,' he says. 'Terry came in wanting to change things and maybe in hindsight now Terry might look back and think he possibly did that too early. Trevor [Peake] certainly had more in the tank to offer Coventry. Personalities clash, though. Unfortunately for Terry it didn't go as well as he would probably have liked.'

On 6 January 1992, after just over a year in charge, Butcher was sacked. Seasoned coach Don Howe was the safe pair of hands that took over. Howe was already at the club as Butcher's assistant and his brief was to keep the Sky Blues in the top flight ahead of the launch of the Premier League the following year. Club secretary Graham Hover was part of the committee in charge of the launch of the Premier League and he was aware of how important it was that the Sky Blues avoided relegation.

'There was talk of a breakaway and some of the bigger clubs setting up their own league and we didn't know if we would be part of it,' he says. 'We didn't fit in with the Liverpools and the Man Uniteds. It was great to be playing them but when it came to financial muscle we were small fry. We were punching above our weight and had been for a number of years. It was very important we were part of the Premier League.'

Howe achieved his goal and kept City up, but only just, as Coventry survived on goal difference. Howe was slated to stay on and work alongside the new manager, who, incidentally, was also one of the club's old managers, Bobby Gould. However, ahead of the start of the season, Howe, understandably not keen on his lengthy commute from Hertfordshire, walked away from the club. This left Bobby Gould as the sole man at the helm as Coventry City entered the Premier League era. A whole new ball game was on the horizon and, with Bobby in charge, it was going to be explosive.

1.

A Whole New Ball Game

UNORTHODOX. IF you put a gun to my head and asked me to describe Bobby Gould using one word, that would be my choice. I'm not quite sure why anyone would do that, but if it ever happens, the research and interviewing for this book has solidified 'unorthodox' as my pick. Gould did things his own way, as you will see over the next couple of chapters. For starters, they say never to go back, and this wasn't Gould's first dance at Highfield Road. A no-nonsense centre-forward by trade, he was signed by Jimmy Hill, penning his first professional contract in 1964. He went on to score 40 goals in 82 matches before moving on to Arsenal. He returned to Coventry as manager for a spell from 1983 to 1984. Despite the astute, cut-price signings of Steve Ogrizovic, Brian Kilcline and Cyrille Regis, among others, City found themselves scrapping at the wrong end of the table throughout Gould's first spell in charge, and in late 1984 he was sacked.

It was, therefore, a slight surprise that he returned for a second bite in 1992. Here we stood at the dawn of this new era for football and the gaffer who was trusted with leading the club at this time was an ex-manager sacked just a few years earlier. He was also a manager described by many, even in 1992, as 'old school'. However, while some of his methods may have belonged to a slightly bygone era, after the Butcher debacle the club was in need of a lift, and one thing Bobby

Gould can deliver is exactly that. The man bleeds sky-blue blood, too. I first spoke to Bobby for a *Coventry Telegraph* interview back in 2006 and his enthusiasm and passion for the club was remarkable and something that stuck in my head even as I dialled his number for an interview for this book some 16 years later.

On his return to the club, Gould was briefed that, while the Premier League was set to make the game richer than ever, he wouldn't be able to enjoy free spending. Instead, he would need to unearth lower league gems once more. That was no problem, though, as he had a secret weapon.

'The first time I met Bobby, he told me he would show me the future of the football club,' Stuart Linnell recalls of meeting Gould shortly after his first appointment as manager back in 1983. 'He took this little black book out of his pocket. It was full of names of footballers, locations and phone numbers. He went out and signed these players from non-league that none of us had ever heard of, because he thought they were the players who would be hungry and would do a job for the club.'

That little black book would certainly be put to the test in the coming months. The aforementioned trio of Ogrizovic, Regis and Kilcline had been snapped up for pennies during Gould's first reign and all went on to become club legends, so there was optimism that he could repeat the trick. Key signings that summer included John 'The Flying Postman' Williams, snapped up for £250,000, and defender Phil Babb, a relatively big-money acquisition by Gould's standards at £500,000 from Bradford City. This was textbook Gould, signing hungry young players from the lower divisions. Players who otherwise may not have got their chance in the big league. Players who felt a debt to Gould's confidence in them. Players who would run through brick walls for their manager. Gould reveals that they were also players within whom he saw himself.

'I joined Coventry City when I was 15 on the ground staff,' Gould says of his arrival at the club back in the 60s. 'Billy Frith was the manager. I worked and worked, played in the B team, got my nose into the reserves but it wasn't to be. It was a knock-back. I had to get a job as an apprentice heating and ventilation engineer. All of a sudden, Billy Frith got the sack and Jimmy Hill came in and invited all of the local lads back on to the training ground. I had a trial and Jimmy said he liked what I had done and he wanted me to come back that afternoon. I said, "No, I'm not coming back this afternoon Mr Hill, but I'll come back next week." The next Sunday I played in a trial for Jimmy Hill. He liked what he saw and he told me he'd like me to sign as an apprentice. He said, "But before you sign that contract, I want to know why you wouldn't come last Sunday." I told him that my dad, Roy Gould, was going blind and the only opportunity I had to see him was at 2pm on Sundays. He stood there, smiled and said, "You and me are gonna be alright, you know." From there it all just flowed. I went through those tough times, just like the [lower league] players I was looking at when I was a manager. Those players, I had that feeling for them. I felt the spirit that they had. I had spirit, I would never give in and that's what I related to when I would go and watch those players. I had a good assessment of lower league players and putting them into a group. I would say, "Right, you want to play professional football, you want to play in the top division, well here's your opportunity."'

Gould's penchant for lower league talent is near-legendary, not least because he helped to launch the career of one of English football's most iconic figures during his first run in charge at Highfield Road.

'There's the famous story about Stuart Pearce,' says Stuart Linnell. 'He wanted to check him out one more time so told his wife Marge he was taking her out for a meal. She asked where and he told her Stevenage, because that's where Stuart

Pearce was playing on that night. She said, "Oh you're not taking me to another football match!" He told her not to worry because it wouldn't take long – and it didn't. They were there for seven minutes. In that first seven minutes they saw Pearce, fairly, take out his man and deposit the ball in the back row of the stand. Bobby turned to Marge and said, "That's enough for me." They went out for their meal and the following week Stuart Pearce signed for Coventry.'

While Gould's eye for a lower league gem can't be called into question, I must say that during the research and interviewing for this book, I found that players generally fell into one of two camps. Some senior pros were critical of Gould's second spell in charge. On the other hand, many of the players who Bobby brought to the club spoke with incredible warmth, with several describing him as the best manager they had worked for. It's a fascinating split in the camp; at times it seemed like two different dressing rooms were being described. Here, I've done my best to give both sides their say.

Stewart Robson was signed by Terry Butcher from West Ham. A classy, former Arsenal midfielder who had once been on the cusp of a breakthrough for England, his career had been derailed by injuries and he had spent much of the few years before his arrival at Highfield Road on the treatment table rather than the pitch. After impressing in a short loan spell, Robson signed a permanent deal with Coventry and immediately slotted into the middle of the park. A player-of-the-year winner in his debut season with the club, Robson was enjoying his time in Coventry, but that was about to change.

'I was really enjoying my football and decided that I wanted to spend a long time at Coventry,' he says. 'Unfortunately, the manager changed. With that, my good feeling towards the club changed. I had a lot of praise from all quarters in that first season [1991/92]. Bobby Gould came in and his first words to me were that I had too much influence on the club and he was going to change that.'

The cultured midfielder believes that Gould had a simple way of lessening his influence – by selling him.

'I was getting phone calls from Tottenham and Aston Villa asking if I would be interested in going there,' he says. 'I challenged Bobby about this and he said he wanted me at the club but he was just seeing what my value was. I said I wanted to stay at Coventry, I loved it and had settled in. I knew he wanted me out. I knew I wasn't his kind of character. I was maybe a bit too strong for him at the time. It was a shame because it was such a good season the previous season and I had loved every minute of it.'

Meanwhile, long-serving full-back Brian Borrows wasn't a fan of the direct style of play that Gould introduced.

'I didn't really see the game the way Bobby saw it,' says Borrows. 'We'd been coached with John [Sillett], and Terry to a degree, where it was build-up play, we'd get the ball, we'd play it to feet, we'd get it to Cyrille and we'd go from there. Bobby's thoughts on the game were to just get it forward as quick as possible and almost play percentage football. I found that difficult. I'd been brought up at Everton and playing it out from the back. I'd like to think one of my main attributes was on the ball and I found it quite difficult under Bobby.'

Robson was another who didn't share Gould's vision of the game. The midfielder claims that the team's tactical approach during pre-season was to play the ball on the ground, to pass and move with pace. He reckons, however, this all changed when it came to the opening match with Middlesbrough.

'The strange thing was in pre-season he never mentioned long-ball,' he recalls. 'In pre-season we were passing the ball around. We got to the opening weekend against Middlesbrough and he told us what he wanted and what he expected. No more than two touches in midfield. I questioned why we had done pre-season as we had and now we were doing this. As Bobby would, he would say, "Just do as I say." There's nothing wrong with long-ball football but don't hide it behind something else. If you play long-ball well it can be effective, as it was in the opening weeks of the season. It got the best out of John Williams and Peter Ndlovu.'

That it most certainly did. While some players may not have agreed with Gould's methods, there's no denying that they worked, as City started the 1992/93 season in fantastic form. The Sky Blues kicked off the campaign with wins over Middlesbrough, Spurs and Wimbledon to sit proudly at the top of the Premier League table. The Premier League billed itself as a whole new ball game, and it seemed to be a game that Gould was more than equipped for.

Team	P	GD	Pts
1. Coventry	3	+4	9
2. Norwich	3	+3	7
3. QPR	3	+3	7

'We were surprised at how well we started but we then just realised that you don't have to be household names to be successful,' says Robert Rosario, a striker signed by Butcher, but a player who flourished under Gould. 'It just clicked and worked with us. It was a changing of the guard with the young guys getting chances, like Peter Ndlovu, John Williams and Lee Hurst.'

For others it was the same old game, despite the influx of flash and pizazz from the broadcasters.

'The Premier League felt like just another season under a different name,' says Micky Gynn. 'The only difference was that now you had all of these dancing girls before a TV match [laughs]. We won our first three games so that was a great start. We beat Spurs 2-0 but I missed a penalty. It was the first penalty to be missed in the Premier League, so I've got that claim to fame. It was on my 31st birthday as well.

John Williams scored both goals that day and we beat them comfortably. That sent a message, to beat Spurs away like that, it should have been three or four. John was a very underrated player. He was a breath of fresh air that season.'

'I had supported Spurs since I was seven years old,' goalscorer Williams says. 'I just wanted to play well. I left a little mark in their head that night. The second goal, everyone raved about how special it was, but that was my trademark goal. I scored lots of goals like that at Swansea because that's what I was engineered to do. The ball came through, I ran from the halfway line and left the defenders in my wake and slotted it right into the corner from an acute angle. They called us a route-one team but the move leading to the penalty was a passing move of the highest class. Because it was Gynny's birthday they got him to take the penalty. I don't think they trusted me to take it but, on the night, I think I would have scored because I was on a high.'

Williams certainly seemed to be a signing right out of the Bobby Gould scrapbook. He was known as the Flying Postman due to his victory at the Rumbelows Sprint Challenge, a race held before the 1992 League Cup Final to find the Football League's fastest player. Obviously, the fact that he used to be a postman also played a part in the nickname.

'People don't remember that I scored 13 Premier League goals in my first season, but winning a race at Wembley made me a superstar!' says Williams of his claim to fame. 'I played at Darlington [for Swansea] and it was my friend Jon Ford's birthday. We got back to Watford at about midnight because he only had this rubbish little Mini Metro. We went into the Hilton and, as it was Jon's birthday, we thought we'd go for a drink. We had a glass of champagne and carried on drinking. I got back to my room at about 4am. I was hammered. All the other players were being professional and were tucked up in bed before the race the next day. I was thinking, "It's only a race, who cares?" Next morning, I was asleep in the bath so

Fordy turns on the shower to wake me up. I go to grab him and he runs out shouting, "We're late, we're late!" I got in the shower, got my kit on and got in the lift with Keith Curle. It was me, Jon, Keith Curle and Keith's wife with all of these Man United fans around him. Keith had scored against them in the week and stuck his fingers up at them. They were spitting at him and trying to punch him. I think that affected him in the race. I was still really drunk. In the final, everyone went down into the blocks like in a proper race but in my head I knew if I got down there I was not going to be able to get back up. The gun for the race goes off and everyone gets off before me. I thought if I could catch them by halfway I'd win because I was faster once I got going. Well, the rest is history. I won £10,000 for 11.43 seconds' work.'

Williams netted three goals in the first two matches of the season, justifying the faith placed in him by Gould almost instantly. The manager had spotted the speedy striker while he was still in charge of West Brom.

'We were beating Swansea at The Hawthorns,' Gould recalls. 'This big, lanky fella was playing for Swansea and he had all this pace. We were coasting and all of a sudden this fella caused us all kinds of problems with his pace.'

'West Brom were hotly tipped for promotion at the time,' Williams remembers. 'I was pretty raw but pretty quick. The manager Frank Burrows told me to just go out there, do what I did and cause mayhem. West Brom were 2-0 up. The West Brom fans were all singing, thinking they were getting promoted, and all of a sudden I made three goals from three long balls over the top and we won 3-2. Afterwards, the fans were calling for Bobby's head and the next week they had a coffin at the ground with RIP Bobby Gould on it! Bobby said he couldn't believe the impact that I had in such a short amount of time on the pitch.'

The big lanky fella began the season working perfectly in tandem with another quick attacker with great balance, Peter

Ndlovu. Spotted years earlier by Sillett and signed for just £10,000, the Zimbabwean quickly made a name for himself thanks to his electric pace and eye for a special goal.

'Peter came and in his first training session he was diving all over the place,' Gynn recalls of Ndlovu's arrival in 1991. 'Nobody had touched him and he was diving on the floor. [Sillett] said to him, "Get yourself up, don't start diving around in training." He was such an exciting player. He could go past players without a problem.'

It was a dive of a different kind that Ndlovu was more accustomed to by the time 1992/93 rolled around. He showed this with a stooping headed goal before an assist for Lee Hurst that helped City to a 2-1 win over Sheffield Wednesday in what was the third of a four-match away-winning run.

We've already established that Stewart Robson and Bobby Gould didn't exactly see eye to eye, but Robson is quick to admit that Gould got it right with the man known by some as the Bulawayo Bullet.

'Peter Ndlovu wouldn't have been at the club if Don Howe was still the manager,' says Robson. 'They had got frustrated with him and didn't believe in him, really. He wouldn't have been anywhere near the team come the start of that season. Bobby saw something in Peter Ndlovu that other people didn't and he got the best out of him. He praised him and praised him and made him feel a million dollars.'

'It's like the Jimmy Hill thing with me, you look at people differently,' Gould says of his trust in Ndlovu. 'He had the balance and the blend. He just rocked, when he took someone on he would rock and still have good balance. There was only one place where he had to go and that was in the first team.'

The Gould–Ndlovu love-in was certainly mutual.

'Bobby Gould was like a father to me,' the Zimbabwean attacker says. 'I remember one interview, and I still have this interview, he said if Peter Ndlovu was English he would be in the national team. He said that he would pay to watch me train. He was a strict father, a strict coach, he said he gave me the platform to play so I had to perform and not take that for granted. He coached me and loved me like a son. I remember one game, I'd had a terrible first half. He said to me, "What are you doing?" As we were going out for the second half I just said to him, "Watch this." I played my heart out. I came in at full time and he said, "That's the Peter Ndlovu I know."'

While the team were impressing on the pitch, there was to be an early season casualty in Micky Gynn. He was sidelined for three months after tearing ankle ligaments during the team's first defeat of the campaign, a 1-0 loss against QPR. The Sky Blues lost just two of their first 12 league matches, but there was a blip in the League Cup as lowly Scarborough overturned a 2-0 Coventry win in the first leg with a 3-0 thumping to dump City out. In the league, while certainly difficult to beat, Gould's men were notching up plenty of draws, a problem perhaps due to a lack of a clinical striker. Thankfully, the boss's little black book had an answer for that.

'I was with Pete Robbins and I said I needed a natural goalscorer,' Gould recalls. 'I needed someone that was going to live in the penalty box. I negotiated a deal with [Mick Quinn] from Newcastle. He sat in the office at Ryton and we had a good chat. I said I loved being in the six-yard box when I played and I saw him as a player who was going to score goals for us.'

Quinn has, in the years since, made no secret of his love of playing for Newcastle and it's likely that his first choice would have been to have stayed on Tyneside and fired the Geordies to promotion that season. But Kevin Keegan had other ideas.

'Keegan called me into the office at Newcastle and said Coventry wanted me,' Quinn recalls. 'I had a long chat with Kevin and the gist of the conversation was that I wasn't going to be a regular in the team there. Within a couple of hours I was getting on the motorway to Cov. Bobby said they had a young team, they played some good football, they just needed to put the ball in the back of the net. He said I was the missing piece.'

However, there was one potential sticking point in the signing of Quinn that wasn't jotted down in the little black book but emerged during that first meeting.

Gould continues, 'He said he had to tell me that he'd backed us to go down! We both sat there, just laughing. He said, "You expect me to go score all of these goals and I've backed you to go down!"'

Quinn, or Sumo as he was affectionately known by fans for his slightly larger than typical frame for a top-flight athlete, instantly proved that he was the great goalscorer that Gould had been looking for. He notched an incredible ten goals in his first six matches after his move from Newcastle. His arrival also proved a boon for Robert Rosario. The striker had struggled since his £600,000 transfer from Norwich in 1991, particularly as he had been labelled as the much-loved Regis's replacement. Suddenly, with Quinn as the focal point, Rosario dropped into a slightly deeper role and quickly developed a deadly understanding with his roly-poly partner.

'Quinny was one of the most unbelievably natural goalscorers there has ever been,' Rosario says of his partner. 'The guy didn't care what he looked like, he could just score goals in his sleep. God gave him that gift. We made each other better. For clubs like Coventry you need that chemistry because you don't have the same budget as the big guys.'

'Micky Quinn coming in, when you saw him you thought he didn't really look the part, not an athlete,' Stewart Robson adds. 'He was a bit of a Jack-the-lad, but a lovely bloke. He was obviously a good finisher. You were so surprised how he managed to find the space or hold off a challenge. He was a perfect fit for Bobby Gould. He was a little bit unconventional, lived on confidence, a bit mad at times but a very good finisher and knew how to find space in the box. He gave the club a lift.

He got more out of players around him, like Robert Rosario, and Ndlovu was flying down the wing.'

Ndlovu *was* flying down the wing, although sometimes Quinn wasn't exactly sure where the Zimbabwean would end up.

'Peter would drive me absolutely fucking potty!' Quinn laughs. 'He would beat 15 players, I'd be waiting in the box and all he'd have to do was roll it back to me for a tap-in and he'd try to bend it around 19 people to score. Then he'd beat 19 people and lash one in the top corner. He was an explosive player. As a character, I took a shine to him, he was bubbly all the time, very skilful and he was a match-winner. He could create a goal out of nothing, he was a top player.'

Quinn's goals were all well and good but, despite bagging six in his first four matches, his efforts failed to inspire City to a single victory, instead falling to a 3-2 defeat against Manchester City, followed by three draws. After 19 matches of the season, the Sky Blues had slipped from early season table toppers to tenth, having been leapfrogged by the likes of Manchester United, Aston Villa, Norwich and their next opponents, Liverpool. Quinn again was on song and so were his team-mates as Graeme Souness's men were swept aside in a thrashing.

The pre-match signs, however, didn't look promising. Coventry would be missing the calming experience of Steve Ogrizovic in goal due to injury and were forced to call upon a rookie to make his debut. Gould was fully aware of what that particular rookie could do, as it was his son Jonathan.

'It was a dream,' the younger Gould says when discussing his ascension to the first team. 'I woke up on the morning of the Liverpool game not thinking I was playing. I got a phone call from the manager, my father, saying Oggy had hurt his neck and I'd be making my debut against Liverpool that afternoon.'

A father and son link-up within a club may be relatively unusual but, in fact, Coventry saw the same thing a few years later as Gordon Strachan's sons Gavin and Craig buzzed around the fringes of the first team. During the interviews for this book, both Bobby and Jonathan mentioned the word nepotism. They clearly share concerns that those on the outside, or perhaps even those within the club, harboured thoughts that Jonathan may have been fast-tracked into the team. In fact, Jonathan suspects that, perhaps due to that fear of nepotism in the back of his mind, his dad was harsher on him than the rest of the squad. One thing his team-mates certainly had going for them over their young goalkeeper was that they could escape the gaffer after a poor performance. Not so for Jonathan, who was still living in the family home when he broke into the first team.

'There were times when I was a little bit petulant and the hammer would come down harder on me,' he says. 'Nepotism isn't a very nice word and I struggle with it. If my dad had been a butcher and I had joined the business, then it would have been Bobby Gould Butchers and Son. It just followed that my grandfather was a footballer, my dad, me and my son also. There were some challenges when I was living at home. I was told to move out a couple of times! As a player you're home before the manager, so I'd be home after a match, settled in front of *Home and Away* or *Neighbours* and he'd come in and his scowl would be there after a defeat. That was the point when we both felt it was best for me to move out.'

It's safe to assume that Jonathan was able to enjoy *Neighbours* in peace after his debut performance, as he proved himself a more than able deputy when Liverpool came to Highfield Road six days before Christmas in 1992. The visitors started the better and Gould was by far the busier of the goalies for much of the first half. Then, on 37 minutes, Jamie Redknapp felled Lee Hurst in the box and Brian Borrows dispatched the resulting penalty with supreme confidence. The ball shot into the roof of the net, more by accident than design, it later transpired.

'To be honest, I didn't quite mean to put it right in the top corner,' Borrows admits. 'I wanted it that side of the goal but even I had a little bit of a scare as it just went under the bar.'

If the first goal was a thunderous effort, the second was a real rocket. Borrows was again the scorer, lashing home after a clever free kick that looked fresh from the training ground but, as with the penalty, looks can be deceptive.

'The second goal wasn't rehearsed,' Borrows says. 'Kevin Gallacher was on the free kick and just saw me a few yards to the side. He rolled it across to me and I took a shot. It found its way into the corner of the net. It was just off the cuff. It must be the only game where I ever scored two goals! Everything that we touched seemed to go in that night.'

The change between the sticks wasn't the only difference that day. Rosario proudly wore the captain's armband for the first time. He admits that it came as a shock to everyone, most of all himself and his poor, unaware mum in the crowd.

'I'd never been a captain before,' he says. 'Robbo was injured and then Oggy was injured so we were sitting in the changing room and Gouldy looked at me and said, "Hey, you're going to lead the team out today." I thought he was messing around. He sat next to me and said, "You don't realise what a leader of men you are." I said I'd never been a captain before and he said, "You're a leader." To be captain against Liverpool at home; wow. I usually came out of the tunnel at the back, and I led us out and I saw my mum in the crowd mouthing, "What are you doing?" I looked up and shrugged my shoulders! I think I got three assists that game and man of the match. It was textbook Gouldy, he was so left of centre. He was a little bit old school but not set in his ways. He was like Cloughie, where he was different. The players loved Gouldy. I loved that man.'

The new skipper played in Gallacher for the third of the night, before Redknapp pulled one back with a stunning free kick that wouldn't have been stopped even if City had both

Gould and Ogrizovic in goal. Redknapp's eventful evening took a turn moments later, however, as he was sent off for a foul on Gallacher. From there, that man Quinn got in on the act and bagged a brace. It ended Coventry 5 Liverpool 1. Scouser Quinn was delighted to have got one over his boyhood team, even if his family weren't quite so keen.

'I brought my dad and uncles down for the game, they're all Liverpool fans,' he says. 'They thought, "Let's hope our Mick has a good game but we hope Liverpool batter them." That was one of our best all-round games as a team and *we* battered *them*. I put the cream on top of the cake with my two, the last two of the game. I was buzzing afterwards. I got to the players' lounge and saw my dad and uncles and they had faces as long as Ruud van Nistelrooy's! I gave them a right bollocking.'

It wasn't just goals that Quinn brought to the team. Throughout my work on this book I've heard from numerous players and managers about the importance of the spirit in the dressing room. By all accounts, Coventry had a great blend of characters in the camp for much of the 90s. Quinn's addition to this particular dressing room was certainly a positive one.

'Micky came in and was like a breath of fresh air,' Micky Gynn assesses. 'Over his whole career he's scored loads of goals. He's not someone who's going to outrun many defenders but get the ball into the box and he was as sharp as a tack. He was a great character. I remember when we played Norwich in the cup in midweek and then we were playing them in the league three days later, so we decided to stay over there in a hotel rather than driving home and back again. Mick organised a table tennis competition between the players. He was the bookie. On the quiet, I said "Listen Quinny, I guarantee I can win this competition because I'm pretty good at table tennis." I'd won a competition years before at Peterborough United. I'm built like a table tennis player, quite short with good backlift. Some lads put some money on me.

I got to the final against Jonathan Gould and beat him quite comfortably. Me and Quinny cleared up with the betting because I'd given him that inside information!'

'What a character,' Brian Borrows continues. 'He was probably the most unfit player I played with but he was the best finisher. He was the most obsessive finisher. Whether it be in training or a five-a-side, all he was interested in was scoring goals. It's a shame we didn't get him in the top division when he was younger and in his prime. We got him towards the end of his career. Imagine having him in the Sillett era, up front with Cyrille Regis.'

It wasn't just his fellow players that were quickly seeing the benefits of Quinn's arrival. He became an almost instant fan favourite. I was only seven years old at the time, but distinctly remember being in awe of this heavy-set goal machine. The local media also picked up on the moustachioed goal-getter.

'He's fat and round and scores at every ground!' Stuart Linnell laughs. 'He was the fastest man over a yard that you'll ever see. He had a point to prove. He felt he hadn't been given a fair deal previously in football. Here he was, given a chance by Bobby Gould, who he still calls gaffer, by the way! He holds him in high regard because he gave him that chance. I think Bobby probably identified with Micky a little bit, they were in a similar mould.'

You'd expect a 5-1 thumping of Liverpool to be the highlight of any season in Coventry's history, but just one week later they pulled an equally momentous result out of the bag. This time Aston Villa were the visitors to Highfield Road. Gould's men served up a Christmas cracker. Their preparation was typically unorthodox for a Bobby Gould team.

'On Boxing Day when we beat Villa, before the game [assistant manager] Phil [Neal] took us for a run around outside the stadium,' Rosario recalls. 'It was snowy and icy and we were running around the stadium. We thought he was out of his mind, it was embarrassing! Maybe it worked though.'

Brian Borrows, meanwhile, recalls a walk across the snow-covered Stoke Park grass with Gould prior to kick-off. Whichever way you slice it, trudging through snow and ice isn't your typical warm-up for a match against your local rivals. It did the trick though. Coventry romped to a 3-0 win. Quinn bagged the first with a neat, hooked finish, before he added a second from a Rosario cross. The duo linked up again to complete the scoring, this time Quinn assisting Rosario to make it 3-0.

'Highfield Road, when it was full, was incredible and had a fantastic atmosphere that day,' says Quinn of the Villa match. 'It could be very intimidating. Me and big Rob were on great form. The first goal, Hursty played it to Robert, he flicked it on and I hit it as sweet as a nut with my left foot. It was a guided volley, it wasn't about power, it was precision.'

The result meant that, at the halfway point of the season, Coventry were seventh in the table, just eight points behind surprise league leaders Norwich. If anyone was getting carried away, the trip to Old Trafford that came next brought everyone back to earth with a bump. After witnessing the Sky Blues humble two of their title rivals, Manchester United weren't going to underestimate Bobby Gould's men.

'I remember being very nervous on the day,' says Jonathan Gould, who was once again in goal. 'My dad said to me in the dressing room at Old Trafford, "If you can keep the ball out of the net for the first 20 minutes, we've got a chance." We were on a bit of a run ourselves. Well, Giggs put one in the top corner and Mark Hughes put one in the bottom corner and we came in at half-time 2-0 down. Dad looked at me as if to say, "I did say about the first 20 minutes," and I countered by saying, "I think it was 23 and 25 minutes that they scored their goals!"'

A 5-0 hammering was certainly a setback, but the team were still comfortably in the top half of the table at the start of 1993. That's not to be sniffed at after a final-day escape to stay in the division the previous year. The excellent form can be attributed to the goalscoring prowess of Quinn, but it's also difficult to ignore the spirit and game plan that Gould had put into place. Despite not being every player's cup of tea, the 11 on the pitch were doing the job set for them and doing it well. Gould had showed faith in Ndlovu, which had been richly rewarded. He had also signed a pair of bargains in Williams and Babb, while the likes of Rosario and Hurst were in the form of their lives. No doubt buoyed by this excellent run, it was around this time that my dad decided to take me to my first match. On 30 January 1993, I sat in the Family Stand and watched what was, quite frankly, a diabolical game of football. We lost 2-0 to Wimbledon, going behind as early as the fourth minute, having been undone by a goal from the archetypal 90s football playboy, Dean Holdsworth. Not the start to my match-attending career that I, or my dad, would have hoped for, but I was at least off and running. More importantly, we got back to winning ways a week later with a 2-0 win away at Middlesbrough and all once again looked rosy.

It wasn't to last, unfortunately. In late April, with the team riding high in the table, Rosario was sold to Nottingham Forest. Judging by goals alone, many thought the striker wouldn't be a big miss. He had bagged just four goals all season. But his presence and link-up play had benefited the likes of Gallacher, Ndlovu, Williams and, especially, Quinn.

'I'm aware people said I didn't score enough goals and I fully agree with them, but if we had assists like they do now, I guarantee I'd have been top of the assists league every single year,' he asserts. 'Whether it was with Kevin Gallacher, Quinny or at Norwich and Forest, I've always been a team player. I didn't score a lot of goals but my team-mates scored – I made them millionaires because I created a lot of chances. My team-mates like Quinny loved me because of that and I loved them too.'

31

Rosario had battled through a difficult time under Terry Butcher to make himself a key part of the first-team picture. Not only that but he was clearly loving his time at the club and had no desire to leave.

'My first year at Coventry was miserable,' he admits. 'People looked at me like I was coming in to replace Cyrille, which wasn't the truth. That first season with Terry Butcher was difficult because of that. The greatest thing for me that ever happened was Bobby Gould coming to the club. He is, and will always be, my favourite manager. He was a player's manager. He was smart, funny, tough, but so respected. He put together a good team on a small budget. Under Bobby I went from the most miserable time of my career to my favourite time. Phil Babb, Andy Pearce, Lee Hurst, Quinny – I loved them all. We weren't big names but we played for each other and had a great chemistry. I'd play centre-back, centre-midfield, up top – I'd have done anything for that team.'

The striker reckons it was Gould's ability to spot a player and bring them successfully into the fold that had propelled the Sky Blues from relegation battlers to a team on the hunt for Europe.

'Bobby would do some tactical stuff in the week but before the game and at half-time, that's when the coach earns their money,' he says. 'It's all about how they motivate. That's what separates the coaches from the great coaches. Bobby was successful at Wimbledon for a reason. He had a special gift where he could get a shoestring budget and put together a team of misfits and nobodies and make them successful. That's a special person.'

But, with pressure to balance the books seemingly always rearing its head in the background, Rosario was sold to Nottingham Forest in a £450,000 deal. The news was broken to him in typically unusual manner.

'Getting sold to Forest was the worst thing ever,' he says. 'I was training and Bobby called me in. He said, "Sit down. We've sold you. Don't say anything, pack your stuff and get out of here." I didn't want to go. He said it was out of his hands, he was nearly in tears. So was I. I went into the dressing room with Babb and Hurst and told them they'd sold me. They couldn't believe it. That was it. I was gone and I was heartbroken. I was a captain and we were flying. It was my most cherished time.'

Almost 30 years on, Gould is honest in his assessment of exactly why he had no choice but to move a first-team regular on.

'You have to look at the financial situations at the club,' he says. 'In those days we were only owned by one individual, not like the finances you see now. Now you see £26m, £38m, £42m – god, if I'd had that money I'd have really spent it well. Football clubs were then just owned by one person and that one person had to financially make sure everything worked and we didn't drown.'

For Quinn, losing his strike partner was a huge blow and one that he still struggles to see the sense in.

'Robert was very unselfish,' he says. 'He wasn't a natural goalscorer like myself so he would run the channels, hold the ball up, flick it on and I'd be in the box getting on the bits and pieces. He was sold for a pittance, which pissed me off. Bobby didn't want him to go but financially, according to the chairman, we were skint. What a waste of what we could have achieved. I never really got the service after that, it was a rotation of strikers to play up front with. It was never quite the same after he went. That was a massive turning point for me. Bobby would say to me to not get back for corners, just to stay up front, get in that box and, while Robert was there, that was what happened and I was scoring goals left, right and centre.'

Rosario left in early March 1993 with the Sky Blues fifth in the table. While the top three of Aston Villa, Manchester United and Norwich had, in all honesty, pulled away from the rest of the league, fourth-placed Sheffield Wednesday were only ahead of City on goal difference. A top four finish was not only a possibility, but it was well within reach.

Team	P	GD	Pts
3. Norwich	30	0	53
4. Sheffield Wednesday	30	+6	46
5. Coventry	31	+5	46
6. Blackburn	30	+11	45

However, the club notched just two wins in the remaining 12 matches of the season, with Quinn scoring only three goals in that time. The entire team managed a mere eight goals in those fixtures, with three of them coming in a final-day draw against Leeds. The sale of Rosario was compounded just a few weeks later as the popular Kevin Gallacher moved to Blackburn in a player-plus-cash deal that saw Roy Wegerle move in the opposite direction.

'We should have kept Kevin,' believes Micky Gynn. 'I don't know what the club was doing, really. You can't keep selling your best players. Eventually that caught up with the club.'

The drop-off in form saw City fall like a stone to a disappointing 15th by the time the season ended. While many attributed this to the loss of Rosario and Gallacher, others believed that the club had simply been punching above its weight in the first half of the campaign. Peter Ndlovu's form tailed off slightly in the mid-season period as well, which also contributed. Stewart Robson, who had been in and out of the team in an injury-disrupted term, suggests that such peaks and troughs were inevitable under Gould's stewardship.

'Bobby is the sort of manager where when things are going well everybody is great, the world is great and that builds up momentum so you might win four or five games on the trot,' he explains. 'When you lose one he goes into screaming and shouting and you lose six or seven on the trot. He'd be high on emotion when you were winning and then at the bottom of the world when things were going wrong. That manifested into the performances you got week to week.'

Others, meanwhile, believe that the 1992/93 Coventry squad lacked that vital ingredient that separates the top teams from the also-rans – consistency.

'Consistency is a key word at any level,' says Brian Borrows. 'Any team can win a cup game and have a giant-killing, but what matters is being able to consistently put results together. That word consistency will never go away in football. The best teams and players are consistent and give you eight out of ten every week. The weaker players might be a nine one week and then a four the next.'

A season that had shown so much promise ended on something of a down-note. However, fans had been treated to some of the finest results since Sillett's reign. For starters, walloping Liverpool and the Villa, and there was also a 5-2 victory over free-spending Blackburn, showing that there was plenty to smile about. After a drab couple of years, there were heroes to believe in again at Highfield Road. The electric pace of Ndlovu and Williams, and Quinn's razor-sharp finishing going forward. In the middle of the park, Robson and Hurst looked a classy combination, while at the back, Babb was growing in stature by the day. In a tightly packed league table, City finished just three points above the relegation zone but also only seven away from Liverpool in sixth. A big summer was ahead for Gould if he was to get his team back firing in time for the 1993/94 season. When the fixture list arrived, it showed that a trip to Highbury against George Graham's Arsenal was to be Coventry's opening assignment of the new campaign. A tricky trip, for sure, but it was to prove to be one of the most memorable matches of the club's entire Premier League stay.

2.

Quinny Does the Wright Thing

AFTER THE disappointing end to the previous campaign, the Sky Blues needed a lift as they prepared for the 1993/94 season. Bobby Gould, of course, had his own slightly off-the-wall idea for how to boost spirits in the camp. Modern-day pre-seasons for top-flight clubs might involve jetting off for commercially lucrative matches in the US or Far East. They may just as easily entail a jaunt around Europe, picking up match fitness while soaking up the sun. Back in the summer of 1993, however, the Sky Blues chose a very different approach. Gould's Coventry made the trip to an Aldershot army barracks to be put through their paces on gruelling assault courses. Players were up at 6am and left to pitch their own tents and prepare food, with lights out by 10pm.

It was a typically bonkers start to the season from Gould, and one that several players have spoken warmly of.

'Bobby was a good character,' says defender Peter Atherton. 'We went down to the army camp – that was an experience. I still talk to players I coach now about that experience. We shot rifles, we were up at six in the morning in the full army regalia. We did a race on a hot July day and you had to work as a team and it was a race between three groups while you had gas masks on – it was character-building.'

What was character-building for some was not an ideal use of pre-season to others. Several senior pros voiced their discontent at the trip, with Kenny Sansom allegedly among those refusing to even attend. Stewart Robson freely admits that he wasn't a subscriber to Gould's way of thinking and he wasn't a fan of the manager's choice on this one. Brian Borrows is another who could have done without the trip, particularly as he was nursing an injury at the time.

'It wasn't my cup of tea,' he says. 'I was injured, I'd done my ankle in pre-season. I'd rather have not gone. I'm not sure whatever Bobby had done would have appealed to me but that certainly didn't. I understand why he did it, for team bonding, but it wasn't for me.'

While some have spoken of the team-building that happened during the trip, it certainly had its share of troubles. In his autobiography, Gould speaks of his son Jonathan choking and needing to be resuscitated after a drill involving players wearing gas masks as they navigated through narrow tunnels. While the young goalkeeper recovered fairly quickly from his brush with death, there would be longer-lasting consequences for midfielder Lee Hurst. Hurst ruptured his cruciate ligament while jumping from a high obstacle. Unfortunately for Hurst, the injury spelled the end of his football career. He tried in vain to return, but announced his retirement three years later, having never played for the club again.

'Lee was a good lad,' Micky Gynn recalls. 'His career was cut short by a knee injury and that was down to us going to the army camp. It was a strange decision to go to an army camp. It wasn't a place for footballers.'

While it didn't quite have the desired impact, there's no doubting that the army barracks trip was some thinking outside of the box from Gould. Borrows recalls that the manager was ahead of his times in several ways. The defender mentions Gould being ahead of the curve in employing a sports scientist and his work with strength and conditioning. He was also something of a trailblazer in inviting a psychologist into the club. Borrows is of the mind, though, that psychologist-client confidentiality was perhaps not quite what it should have been.

'Bobby said to all of the players that everything [discussed with the psychologist] would be in confidence,' he says. 'It was worked out, though, that whatever was said in the sessions got back to Bobby. Players started to feed the psychologist false stuff that would get back to Bobby. It became a bit of a joke. You'd have people whistling "The Twilight Zone" when the guy walked down the corridor. Players were quite closed-minded to be honest, not like now where we realise that psychologists can be very useful. It was probably quite forward-thinking from Bobby but we didn't quite maximise what the psychologist could do.'

In the dugout alongside Gould once again for the 93/94 season was Phil Neal. Neal had been appointed as assistant manager during the previous season and continued to juggle the role with his work as part of Graham Taylor's coaching set-up with England. While Neal's coaching credentials seemed sound, he wasn't to the taste of Stewart Robson.

'In my view [Bobby] didn't make a very good appointment in his assistant,' he says. 'Phil rubbed people up the wrong way and was very much a yes man to Bobby. I didn't get on with Phil. We didn't see eye to eye. He was a top player but he was never injured. Any player that was injured, he was wondering what they were playing about at. I had massive rows with him. For me to play for Coventry, I'd had to have two years of rehabilitation work to play football again. He didn't seem to understand that.'

It's little wonder that the pair were at loggerheads, as Robson recalls the previous season that these massive rows astonishingly turned physical one afternoon in the manager's office.

'I've only ever hit one person in my life – it was Phil Neal,' he says. 'I had an eye problem. It was a worrying time. I'd had this problem before and it had gone but on this day it didn't. It eventually turned out that your eye moves almost on a pulley system and one of the roots where the lever works had become inflamed, so my eye wouldn't work quickly enough. I was seeing double vision. I told Bobby I couldn't play, I couldn't see the ball. They looked at me as if I was mad. Phil Neal said I needed to come out and train. I told him he didn't know what I had been through with injuries. He said to just run through it. I said if he wanted me to do that I would, but he would regret it. I went out and trained and crashed into Peter Ndlovu, went through the back of him. Phil said it was disgraceful. We went back into the Sky Blue Lodge and Bobby called me up to the office with Phil. He asked what that was about and I said I had told them I shouldn't be training. I told them I was working seven hours a day to make sure that, when I was fit, I was ready to play. Phil said he was never injured, this and that. He stood up and I said, "Phil, just keep quiet, I'm talking to the manager now." He walked towards me and I thought he was going to come and have a go at me, so I stood up and punched him. Bobby first asked Phil if he wanted to call the police because that was assault, and the next minute he was saying, "Let's sit down and have a plate of biscuits." That's Bobby to a T.'

Aside from an assistant manager and captain who couldn't stand each other, the near-death of a goalkeeper and a midfielder's career ended by injury, things weren't looking too bad as Coventry entered the new season.

It was a somewhat unspectacular summer on the transfer front, the most eye-catching new addition at Highfield Road being veteran striker Mick Harford, who arrived from Sunderland for £200,000. While not a new signing, having joined Coventry the previous summer, Phil Babb went into 1993/94 with expectations on his shoulders as a first-team fixture.

'I remember him playing for Bradford against West Bromwich Albion,' says Gould of his first encounter with Babb. 'He was the left-sided defender in a back four. [I marked] him down and said he was one for the future. I didn't know I was going to Coventry or that I would sign him. He was a natural defender and a good lad. He was a little bit quiet but we brought him out of his shell. These players had all come through the ranks and they respected each other. There were no superstars and talk of how much money everyone is on. They're just normal people that I have had the opportunity to notice their ability.'

Babb was one who seemed to enjoy himself during the army barracks trip, thanks to some late-night pranks with the ever-mischievous Mick Quinn.

'I remember me and Phil Babb creeping around the camp with a stick,' Quinn says. 'It was pitch black, you couldn't see two inches in front of your nose. We crept up on what we thought was one of the lads, poked them in the back with the stick and said, "Halt, who's there?" They replied, "Phil Neal, assistant manager with Coventry, sir." We said, "At ease, at ease," and fucked off. The next morning, we heard Phil saying, "Fuck me, they're good those army lads, I didn't hear them creeping up on me or anything." He still doesn't know to this day that it was me and Babby taking the piss.'

While things were relatively quiet on the incomings front, there were a couple of outgoings that raised eyebrows. Andy Pearce was sold to Sheffield Wednesday, while FA Cup winner Micky Gynn left the club after ten years. The way that the much-loved midfielder left rankles with him even today some 30 years later.

'My contract ran out,' he explains. 'Bobby basically said to me that I had five minutes to get my boots and go. That wasn't a pleasant way to leave after ten years. It was disgraceful, I thought. I lost respect for him then.'

The opening fixture was a daunting trip to Highbury to face Arsenal. The Gunners were not quite the force they had been in the recent past, or that they would be in years to come, having finished tenth the previous year. They had, however, won both the FA and League Cups in 1992/93 and were tipped for a far better league campaign this time around. Thankfully, Bobby had a trick or two up his sleeve to help thwart Ian Wright, Paul Merson and co.

'I went to watch Arsenal play at Rotherham in a friendly,' he says. 'I noticed certain things and realised that pace was going to burn them alive. Playing away from home, that pitch at Highbury was beautiful to play on. When I knew the first game was there I relished the opportunity of playing them. We played on all the best pitches I could find in pre-season. That helped. We had great confidence with Micky Quinn up front as well. Arsenal sent someone to watch us in a pre-season game. I fucked them. Every 15 minutes we changed our system. The guy who came to see us would have gone back and said, "Jesus wept, they played so many formations I couldn't tell you how they're going to play!"'

Gould had once again pulled off a masterstroke. On the opening day, the Sky Blues produced one of the shock results of the season, humbling Arsenal on their own patch with a 3-0 win. Mick Quinn bagged a hat-trick. The first came from the penalty spot, while the second was a neat backheel from Wegerle and a superb finish. The pair combined again for the third as Quinn beat David Seaman once again to claim the match ball.

Jonathan Gould started in goal that day and he knew his role was to get things moving quickly as soon as he claimed the ball.

'I think Oggy was unavailable for the start of the season so I went into pre-season knowing there was an opportunity,' he recalls. 'I think we were 7/1 to win that game but dad was really positive. He said when they had a corner we'd leave three up front and hit them on the counter. My job was to take the crosses and start the counter-attacks and it really worked. I managed to keep Ian Wright out at one end and Quinny put three past the England keeper at the other end. Tony Sheridan was playing one of his first games in midfield as well and there was a lot of pace and smart footballers in that team.'

Sheridan was given the opportunity to start in midfield in the light of that injury to Hurst. Not that the young Irishman realised that himself in the days before the season kicked off.

'I thought I'd be on the bench because I'd played in a lot of pre-season friendlies,' he says. '[Bobby] walked into the dressing room, named the team and I was in it. He was a great manager. I remember going up to Leeds and making my debut [the previous season]. To be truthful, I never dreamt I would even be on the bench. We'd take 18 players and then name a squad of 16, so I thought I'd be one of the two players in the stand. Literally, we came out of the hotel, he called me to the front of the team bus and told me I was starting – an hour and a half before kick-off. He was one of the best man-managers.'

It wasn't just his spell in midfield that made an impression that day. Mick Quinn recalls Sheridan having the last laugh come full time, as well.

'Ian Wright had his single out, "Do the Wright Thing", and they had leaflets for that everywhere. They had the season before won the FA Cup and League Cup and it was a party atmosphere,' Quinn recalls. 'We definitely spoiled the party. At the end even Wrighty said to me, "Some fantastic finishes, Mick." We were celebrating in our dressing room afterwards and Shez wrote on one of Wright's "Do the Wright Thing" leaflets, "Quinny did the Wright Thing". He slipped it under their dressing room door. We heard George Graham screaming and shouting at the top of his voice about it. Merse got dragged off and George Graham was ripping into him, asking if he had been on the ale the night before, and Merse said, "Well, Quinny was on the ale last night and he got a hat-trick!"'

Quinn treated the Highbury crowd not just to his goalscoring prowess that day, but also his dance moves as he busted out his iconic (or absolutely bloody awful to most non-Sky Blues fans) funky chicken celebration.

'Prior to that game, we went for a night out a couple of weeks before the big kick-off,' Quinn recalls. 'We were out and this old song "The Funky Chicken" came on. We were half pissed and said whoever scored against Arsenal had to do the Funky Chicken dance. When I scored the penalty, I did that stupid fucking dance down the wing.'

Warwickshire lad Nigel Winterburn lined up for Arsenal that day and he accepts that, while the result was unexpected, it was well earned by the Sky Blues.

'You get funny results on the opening day,' he says. 'You can look at how the teams played last season, you can look at the squad on paper but really at the start of a season you're going into the unknown. Those first three or four games, you're just trying to get a level and into a rhythm. If you look at Arsenal's next six games, we won five out of six, so that shows what a good result that was for Coventry. They were just better than us on the day.'

It was Coventry's attacking talent that made a particular impression on Winterburn. It was a bold line-up selected by Gould, with Williams and Ndlovu both starting, as well as Wegerle and Quinn.

'Roy Wegerle had an enormous amount of ability,' Winterburn says. 'Peter Ndlovu was small but had good technical ability and was quick. If you give these guys time to play then they're going to cause you problems, and that's what happened on the day. Micky Quinn was a terrific finisher as well.'

Quinn was appreciated even more by his own team-mates. His opening-day treble lit belief that he could once again fire

City up the table and better his impressive tally of 17 from the previous campaign.

'I'll tell you why Quinny was one of the best finishers; his backlift was short and he had a range of finishes as well,' says Jonathan Gould. 'You couldn't read him. My dad called it the honeypot. He always seemed to be in the triangle of that six-yard box, and if we put it in there, then he would score.'

Quinn took the match ball home with him for his efforts, but he also picked up a record that he still proudly holds to this day.

'There's no striker who had scored a league hat-trick against Arsenal at Highbury in 75 years,' he beams. 'Nobody did it after that either, because they knocked the ground down!'

It wasn't all good, though, on that opening day. The outspoken Robson picked up a knee injury ten minutes into the match. While the away following that day wouldn't have realised the extent of the injury, Robson himself knew straightaway that it was serious.

'I ruptured my cruciate,' he says. 'I knew from the moment I did it that I'd never play again. I can't do anything these days, not on a bike or running. I had the operation to repair my knee and I got an infection. I was in hospital for five weeks and at one point I thought I was going to lose my leg. I had five operations in five weeks. You can imagine what state my leg was in at that point. It was over a year before I was walking properly, so I knew I'd never play again.'

The injury meant that the Sky Blues had lost three of their central-midfield options from the previous year, Robson and Hurst through long-term injury and Gynn, who had been released. This opened the door for the likes of Willie Boland to come in alongside fellow Irishman Sheridan.

'Bobby could pick out the characters that a squad needed in order to be successful,' says Boland on his integration into the squad. 'He bought a lot of players that weren't pulling up any trees at other clubs, brought them to Coventry and brought them together. It's a skill in itself to do that, to bring certain characters in and to make that dressing room successful.'

That's exactly what Coventry had in those opening weeks of the season; a successful dressing room. The Arsenal win started an eight-match unbeaten streak that saw the club sat proudly in the top six in mid-September.

Team	P	GD	Pts
3. Aston Villa	8	+5	15
4. Everton	8	+4	15
5. Tottenham	8	+6	14
6. Coventry	8	+5	14

We're heading back to that buzzword once again here, unorthodox. I've read stories of Bobby's unusual way of encouraging players to sort out their differences. He would suggest players gather around in a circle while the two warring parties sorted their issues in the middle. It was known as 'the circle'. He's spoken of picking up this unusual way of restoring squad harmony from Dave Bassett at Wimbledon, and there's a famous story of Gould himself having a wrestle in the circle while he was Wales manager, with striker John Hartson. With regards to that particular incident, Gould has spoken of looking up while grappling on the floor with Hartson, to see Ryan Giggs and Mark Hughes watching on. At that point he wondered to himself whether the pair would have ever witnessed Sir Alex Ferguson wrestling with one of his players. At Coventry, midfielders Boland and Sheridan both have memories of the circle.

'People would call him old school,' says Boland. 'He addressed problems head-on and that's a skill in man-management in itself. If you have a problem in a dressing room you don't want that spreading and causing negativity. He knew how to manage the dressing room. Listen, there were a couple of times when he would have said, "Go on, up you go the two of you, sort it out and come back to me when it's sorted." He wouldn't be afraid to say that.'

'I did see that one day but nothing came of it,' Sheridan adds. 'He threw down the gauntlet to two players to do that and in all fairness to the two lads they bottled it, left it at that and shook hands. Bobby would get the players around in a circle and say, "There you go, it'll all be done when this is sorted." The two boys were shocked and just went, "Ah, we'll just shake hands and leave it and be on our way."'

Regardless of the methods, Gould was certainly getting the best out of the players he had at the time. Roy Wegerle had joined the previous year in the deal that took Kevin Gallacher to Blackburn, and he had struck up a promising partnership with Quinn.

'Things weren't working out for me at Blackburn,' the American attacker recalls of his move to Highfield Road. 'I wasn't getting on with Kenny Dalglish, he had a different way that he wanted me to play to how I enjoyed playing. I thought Bobby was someone who would have me playing the way I wanted to play, so I went. He had the right words, the right motivation and the passion. He did it all in a way that you could believe. You can't win an FA Cup with Wimbledon without being able to motivate. Bobby gave us a lot of belief but we also had a lot of talented players in our starting 11. We may not have had a big squad, but we had a strong 11. With Micky Quinn, Peter Ndlovu and myself, we had a chance. Micky lacked mobility but he knew where the goal was. Anything that dropped in or around the box, you knew he would finish it. John Williams had a lot of pace and would terrorise defenders with his speed. We had talented players and, with the belief that Bobby instilled in us, that was a good combination.'

Whether you prefer to think of Gould's man-management as old school, from another planet or just straight-up genius, there's no denying that it was doing the trick in the opening weeks of the season. The Sky Blues sat just three points off top spot before a draw with Chelsea and defeats against Leeds and Norwich brought them back down to mid-table. Still, a 1-1 draw with Southampton ended the mini slump and the team looked in decent shape as they prepared to face QPR at Loftus Road on 23 October. It was a match that no one could have predicted the outcome of. An era was about to end at the club, as Bobby entered his final days as Coventry City manager.

3.

Bobby Out ... Phil Neal In

YOU CAN spin statistics different ways, depending on your agenda. Eleven matches into the 1993/94 Premier League season, the Sky Blues had lost just twice. Having said that, only three wins had been picked up, alongside six draws. Still, City were just a point out of the top half of the table and a couple of points behind the hosts for their next match, Queens Park Rangers.

The Sky Blues went into the match without the injured John Williams. Jonathan Gould remained the preferred choice in goal, while Atherton and Babb lined up in defence with full-backs Steve Morgan and Brian Borrows. In midfield it was a mix of youth and experience, with Lloyd McGrath providing some steel alongside Leigh Jenkinson (affectionately referred to as 'the Stepover King' by Williams in interviews for this book), Willie Boland and Sean Flynn, with Ndlovu and Quinn in attack. Borrows had been out on loan at Bristol City but was recalled and started. Midfielder Boland, meanwhile, had been in Sweden with the Irish youth team but was recalled early to play in the match. It would turn out to be one that both probably would have rather missed.

'The game was a disaster,' Boland recalls. 'Les Ferdinand had a field day, he was absolutely brilliant that day.'

Ferdinand scored one, made one and generally proved to be a thorn in Coventry's side in a 5-1 thrashing. To make matters worse, there was on-the-pitch carnage as Peter Atherton suffered a broken cheekbone, yet admirably played on through the pain. Even so, that was nothing compared to the drama that would kick off after the final whistle.

As the players showered, Bobby Gould sought out chairman Bryan Richardson for a chat. The venue that the pair ended up in for their conversation was the gents in the QPR directors' box. It was in these unlikely surroundings that Gould announced he was resigning. It certainly came as a shock to Richardson.

'[Bobby] was ashen white and pouring with sweat in his suit,' he says. 'He said he was quitting. I asked him why and he said we had gone as far as we could go. The next thing I knew, a story appeared in *The Sun* under his name the following week, saying it was down to me because I was going to sell Peter Ndlovu. That was absolutely untrue. Where he got that from, I have no idea. He was very much either 100 or 0, Bob.'

The story of the proposed sale of Ndlovu did the rounds afterwards and seemed to stick for years as the reason for Gould's seemingly knee-jerk decision. However, today Bobby gives a different story, stressing that it was his own error of judgement that led to his departure.

'We were doing well,' he says. 'Prior to going down to QPR, several players wanted to not travel back on the team coach. I said yes to them and all of a sudden we cop a 5-1 defeat. I looked at myself in the mirror and I said, "That is the worst decision you've ever made and you don't deserve to manage this football club." I just felt, there were five goals and it was my responsibility that those players should have had their minds on the game and not what was going to happen afterwards. We weren't on a bad run but sometimes you can get tired, your brain is tired and that was a lack of man-management. We lost 5-1 and I'd have got on that coach to take them back to Coventry and there would have only been five or six of them on the coach – that is diabolical. I wasn't turning around after that. I had the highest respect from them until we got to QPR. I looked at myself and I lacked the power that I should have had and that was it.'

While the reasoning may have left some confusion, it was a typical Gould decision. Here was a man who was 100 per cent at all times, an absolute force of nature. He was either on top of the world or at the bottom of the pile and prone to making calls about his own future that others may fear or deem to be rash. Roy Wegerle recalls taking his post-match shower to the sound of first-team players pleading with Bobby to change his mind, but his decision was final. Some may have been pleased at the prospect of a change, but many players were upset to see the back of the man who had plucked them from the lower leagues or catapulted them from the youth team. The likes of Tony Sheridan, Boland, Williams and Quinn were among those who felt the loss of the gaffer.

'I was gutted,' admits Quinn. 'He was a centre-forward as well and he took me under his wing and gave me a free rein. I was rewarding him for that with the goals. The two turning points for me at Coventry were first when Robert went and then when Gouldy went.'

'Bobby gave me my debut,' Boland adds. 'He looked after me well. He was a good man-manager, he knew how to deal with people. That was his strength. He wouldn't take any messing about. He had experience of working with, you wouldn't say top players, but players at that level who he could get the best out of. He did a really good job. He went too soon.'

With Gould gone, the search for a successor was underway. As it transpired, the club didn't have to look far. Phil Neal was put in temporary charge, knowing that if he could help the club put a run of results together then there was every chance he could take the job on full-time. One of his first decisions was to recall Steve Ogrizovic in goal for his first match in charge, a 0-0 home draw with Sheffield United.

'Whilst my performance against QPR may have warranted [being dropped], my previous performances hadn't,' says Jonathan Gould. '[Phil] felt what had happened to my father would have an impact on me but that's a load of nonsense. I felt I was strong enough of a character to deal with that. I didn't get a look-in then until later on in the season. I don't hold it against Phil, a manager makes decisions and must survive themselves. I'd been at Coventry a long time and loved the club. It's our family club. I didn't want to kick up a fuss, I just got on with it and supported Oggy.'

Gould's attitude of supporting the man with the No.1 shirt was shared by his experienced team-mate.

'You can have three brilliant goalkeepers but only one can play,' Ogrizovic says. 'I've had some great goalkeepers to work with at Coventry and thankfully I was generally given the number-one slot. The goalkeepers who aren't playing are important in supporting the number one and I'd like to think I did that when I wasn't in the team.'

Neal's tinkering did the trick in the short term, with his team picking up wins over Everton and Arsenal, notching a draw with Sheffield Wednesday and falling to narrow defeats against title chasers Blackburn and Manchester United in the following weeks. After the humiliation of shipping five at QPR, Neal had made Coventry difficult to beat. He was rewarded with the manager's job on a full-time basis. Neal started to make his mark at the club immediately, with players noting the differences between their old and new boss.

'Because of Phil's background at Liverpool, he had a totally different style to Bob,' says Dave Busst. 'You could have a chat back with Phil, whereas with Bobby it was, "This is my team, this is how we're going to do it and if you don't then you're out."'

'I got on well with Phil,' adds Brian Borrows. 'We had a comfortable season, that's not to be sniffed at. He was completely different to Bobby. He came from Liverpool and saw the game more like myself.'

He also began gradually overhauling the first team. Midfielder Julian Darby had worked with Neal at Bolton and became the new manager's first signing in a £150,000 deal.

'Bobby resigned and I got a phone call asking if I wanted to come to Coventry,' Darby recalls. 'It was a no-brainer. I was an apprentice under Phil at Bolton and I came into the team and played most weeks. When that happens you're always going to get on with the manager because you've done something for him and he's done something for you. His coaching was enjoyable and he was a very good player. He would join in the games in training and you'd want to be on his team. He was one of the best players, even though he'd retired.'

However, all was not rosy. Some, both players and fans, failed to warm to Neal, no doubt in part due to him being a far less charismatic frontman than Gould. It was also difficult to refute that the team had lost some of the gung-ho excitement instilled by his predecessor. The days of Williams and Ndlovu chasing balls over the top alongside Quinn and Wegerle were drawing to a close. Williams and Quinn, in particular, found themselves cast aside.

'There was a period, I think, he had a month to get the job,' says Quinn. 'We played Everton and Arsenal, where I scored two against Everton and one against Arsenal, and then we drew a game 0-0 and he got the job. I wouldn't mind but I scored the goals and then I never really got a regular look-in with him. It was never the same once Phil Neal took over. Phil was a very good coach but as a manager it's about making big decisions, team selections. I don't think he was a very good manager.'

Williams had been one who Gould had trusted to deliver week in, week out for well over a year, but the new boss came in with different ideas.

'I was doomed when Phil Neal took over,' the pacey attacker says. 'That was the end of my time at Coventry. He was never a fan of mine. I don't know what his problem was. He liked me as a person but I don't think he liked me as a footballer. As a bloke, Phil Neal is a very nice person but I think his man-management skills in dealing with people who weren't of his ilk and hadn't won every trophy going wasn't there. I think the team became predictable in how they played. It was stagnant and boring. It was like watching paint dry. It is a results business and we became hard to beat, but if you can get results and be entertaining then you're a real team. That team reflected Phil Neal's personality.'

As winter fell, things still looked decent enough on the pitch. After the ten-match mark of his reign, Neal had overseen four wins, three draws and three defeats in the league.

Team	P	GD	Pts
11. West Ham	24	-8	33
12. Tottenham	24	+4	30
13. Coventry	22	-1	30
14. Ipswich	23	-5	30

Neal's 11th match in charge is one that I'll always remember as it was my second-ever trip to Highfield Road and my first for the season. The Sky Blues welcomed lowly Swindon, the division's whipping boys, for a night match live on Sky. Roy Wegerle put Coventry one up with just 17 minutes left. That looked to have sealed the points, and my dad and I left the ground on 88 minutes (unfortunately at that point we were the types to 'beat the traffic'). As we skipped down the steps of the West Stand and towards the car my dad stopped dead in his tracks and muttered to himself, 'Are they singing you're not singing anymore?' At eight years old I had no idea what he was on about until we reached the car, turned on the radio and realised that, yes, the Swindon fans were toasting their 89th-minute equaliser with a rendition of 'You're not singing anymore'. Just over a month later we played the return fixture against Swindon and managed to sink to a poor 3-1 defeat. This was a Swindon team known even now as one of the worst to ever play in the Premier League. They picked up just 30 points from their 42 matches, four of which came in two matches with Coventry!

The result came in the midst of a tricky spell for Neal. Form had slipped on the pitch. After picking up 15 points in his first ten matches, City amassed just eight from his next 11. Matters on the field, you would think, can't have been helped by the circus Neal was involved in off it. He was, of course, part of the English national team set-up alongside Graham Taylor. However, the campaign was a notorious flop, with England failing to qualify for the USA World Cup in 1994. This was something Neal was in no mood to exchange banter about.

'When Bobby was manager and Phil was coach he was very good,' says Tony Sheridan. 'I had a bit of banter with him because he was a coach with England and Phil Babb was in the Ireland set-up that qualified for the World Cup. I said to Phil, "Phil Babb will send you back a letter from America," like the [Proclaimers] song. He didn't seem too happy at that, he never put me in the first team afterwards.'

To make matters worse, the qualifying campaign had been filmed for a Channel 4 documentary, which aired for the first time on 24 January 1994, slap bang in the middle of Coventry's poor run. While Taylor was lampooned throughout the campaign, the documentary brought the spotlight on to Neal, portraying him as a monosyllabic yes man, there purely to nod and mumble 'yes boss' to Taylor's every suggestion.

'That documentary just sums him up,' Williams says. 'That's who he was. That was Phil Neal. He's a people pleaser. He would sell himself out just to keep himself in a job. He would say whatever he felt was the right thing to say to the hierarchy. For me, I've got my own views and values. Don't get me wrong, Phil Neal is a legend in this country and in Liverpool, but what he did on that show just showed who he was.'

'That's the way he was,' Sheridan agrees. 'He wasn't under pressure when he was the coach because Bobby was in charge, but when he became in charge that's when I feel the true Phil Neal came out. You can win everything he did as a player but a good player doesn't always make a good manager.'

Whether the man on the screen was the real Phil Neal or not, the situation was very real. Neal had been undermined in the public eye and had become a laughing stock.

'Phil must look back and wince and think, "Oh god, what does this make me look like?"' says Borrows. 'You're leaving yourself up to be ridiculed. You don't know how these things will be edited and I'm sure they painted him in as poor a light as they possibly could. It didn't do Phil any favours.'

One man who was unable to help Neal's cause that season was Roy Wegerle. The attacker's year had been dogged by injury even before he tore his cruciate ligament in January 1994. Wegerle was an important part of the USA national team and, with his home country due to host the World Cup that summer, he was keen to avoid surgery and a lengthy spell on the sidelines.

'I played a lot of the time injured at Coventry,' he admits. 'The physios told me if I had knee surgery I would miss the World Cup and it would take nine months to recover. That wasn't something I was keen on doing. They said I could do my rehab and strengthen my hamstrings as much as I could because that's the back-up for your ACL. They said I'd never get back to 100 per cent, I might get to 70 per cent but at least I'd be able to play in the World Cup. That's what we agreed to do. I never got my knee repaired. I was 31 at the time so the two and a half years at Coventry I was at 70 per cent. I lost a lot of my pace and I couldn't move the ball like I was capable of because my knee wouldn't allow it. Maybe I should have had my knee repaired, taken a year off and come back stronger. I always played on six of my 12 cylinders. Now I look back and I'm disappointed to make that decision but I thought it would be my only chance to play in a World Cup. I wish I had done it because I would have had a better career with Coventry.'

But then, just as quickly as the poor run had started, it ended. After a 1-0 defeat to Leeds on 19 March, the Sky Blues were 13th in the table, eight points clear of the drop zone but having played more matches than several of the teams below them. It wasn't panic stations, but there was some alarm that Coventry could have been that team that drops like a stone in the second half of the season. There needn't have been such concerns. Five wins in the final nine matches of the season, and just one defeat, saw Coventry pull not only well clear of the relegation zone but into the top half of the table. If Neal's task was to steady the ship then it was very much mission accomplished. In signings like Darby and full-back Ally Pickering, Neal was continuing the trend of plucking talents from the lower leagues and sprinkling these hungry up-and-comers alongside established top-flight talent.

'That's what Coventry was then, you had your skilful players like Peter Ndlovu but also the workaholics,' Darby says. 'Players like Dave Rennie, Sean Flynn, Steve Morgan, players who dig in when things get tough and grind results out. Those players had this fantastic opportunity, coming from lower league teams, and it might be their one chance, so they scrapped for their lives. It wasn't always silky football but there was a lot of scrap games and if you win those games then you have a good chance of staying up. At the time our aim was to be on the first page of the league table on Ceefax. If you're on page one of the league table then you're doing brilliantly!'

The result was that on any given day Coventry could match anyone in the division. At the same time they could then go and get hammered by rock-bottom Swindon. This Jekyll and Hyde syndrome is best illustrated by Coventry thrashing Manchester City 4-0 on 19 February of that season before being thumped 4-0 by Newcastle just four days later.

'That was football at that time,' Peter Atherton recalls. 'Anyone could beat anyone. The game has changed so much in terms of things like defensive set-ups. Football was just a bit more free back then. You can get some funny results today but not like back then.'

An undoubted highlight of that fine run-in was welcoming Blackburn to Highfield Road on 2 May. With three matches left, Rovers were still in the title hunt but had to get a result against Coventry, otherwise Manchester United would be crowned champions. The match was live on Sky and they had a camera filming a selection of United players watching the match and would beam back to them throughout to catch their reactions. A brace from Julian Darby helped Coventry to a 2-1 win, and gave Manchester United the title. Sky cut back, probably expecting wild celebrations from the United players, to see an emotionless Paul Parker sat there watching the final seconds of the match – I would have hated to have seen his reaction if Blackburn had won!

A more than creditable 11th-place finish was Coventry's reward after a goalless draw with the champions on the final day.

Team	P	GD	Pts
9. QPR	42	+1	60
10. Aston Villa	42	-4	57
11. Coventry	42	-2	56
12. Norwich	42	+4	53

'I think we overachieved, to be totally honest,' says Willie Boland. 'I think Coventry always overachieved in those years. There were some amazing escapes as well down the years but if you look at the players on the pitch for the last seven games of that season you had myself, Sean Flynn, Dave Rennie, Steve Morgan – none of those bounced off the sheet as being top players. We had a good team ethic and we worked hard. Once you go on a good run it builds confidence. Whether you can sustain that over a whole season, though, is difficult when you're playing against quality players week in, week out.'

While we were almost certainly punching above our weight, there was optimism around the club. A top-half finish and now Neal would have a full pre-season to add to the squad and prepare his troops. What happened next was a surprise to everyone.

The club dragged its heels over offering a new deal to out-of-contract centre-half Peter Atherton, who was subsequently snapped up by Sheffield Wednesday. His defensive partner Phil Babb had earned a glowing reputation, thanks to a fantastic World Cup with the Republic of Ireland, and bagged himself a big-money move to Liverpool. This left Coventry short at the back (Dave Busst jokes that he was the only defender left come the start of the season). With a press conference called to announce a new signing, the gathered media were sure that a centre-half was about to be unveiled. Instead, the club had splashed its record transfer fee on a new striker, Manchester United's Dion Dublin.

'I remember Dion signing and we were all expecting a central defender,' Stuart Linnell recalls. 'Phil Neal comes out with this guy who had been great at Cambridge, signed for Manchester United and had this horrible injury and then never really got his career off the ground at Manchester United. Nonetheless, we knew what he could do, but I said to Phil Neal during the interview that I was surprised he had spent this amount of money on a striker when we needed a central defender. Phil completely ripped into me and told me I was out of order.'

Dublin signed for £1.9m, a big move for the club and one that Neal was nervous about making.

'Phil was really worried about doing the deal because he hadn't had any money before,' Bryan Richardson recalls. 'Dion had only played less than a handful of games for Man United. Mick Brown, Phil's number two, said Dion would be alright. I said to Phil, "Go on, we'll have a gamble on him." We had to do something to get some goals into the team. Martin Edwards was the Man United chairman and he was a good friend and let us pay for Dion over, I think, two years, and that made the deal possible.'

Dublin himself recalls that Neal convinced him that Coventry was the best place for his career to be revived, despite the door still being open at Old Trafford.

'Phil Neal was great,' the talismanic striker says. 'Sir Alex Ferguson didn't want me to leave. He wanted me to stay because back then you could only have three foreign players in Europe, so he said he needed me as one of the British players to play in Europe but if I wanted to go and play regularly then fair enough. He let me go with his blessing. Phil Neal said he needed a focal point, he needed a number nine who could hold the ball up and bring people into play. He said he was happy to pick a team around me more or less, to be honest with you. That is nice, when a manager feels that way about you. Phil sold the move to me.'

Another high-profile addition that summer was American international Cobi Jones. The dreadlocked winger joined the club in a very different kind of deal. This wasn't a transfer from club to club, as the USA didn't have a professional league at the time. The development of the MLS was to be a legacy from the '94 World Cup, but in the interim that left home-grown players kicking their heels. To combat this, the US Football Federation negotiated deals for the players with clubs in Europe, with the understanding that they would return for the commencement of the MLS around 18 months later. The Coventry deal moved into gear when England had played the USA at Wembley earlier in the year but, astonishingly, Jones wasn't part of the discussions himself.

'It was a quick process,' he says of the transatlantic move. 'I couldn't tell you the discussions that the Federation had. I realise that is difficult to understand today but the Federation handled the talks rather than an agent and the player. That would be unheard of nowadays. For me, it was going to the Premier League and having an opportunity to play at the highest level. I was more than happy to do that.'

Today, if a player made a move across the world to a top-flight club, they could expect everything from accommodation and utilities to furnishings and transport to be arranged for them. Back in 1994, this wasn't the case.

'I didn't find it an easy transition,' Jones says. 'The players and fans were great, having Wegerle there helped. One of the biggest issues was figuring everything out. I had someone there with me for the first day and a half and then it was "okay, now you're in the hotel, we'll pick you up in a couple of days". I had to find my own place, figure out where the grocery store was, furnish my own place. I couldn't stay in the hotel forever so I had to find a place to stay. That would never happen today. You need to make yourself comfortable in the situation. I had to figure out bank accounts. Every day after training, when you're exhausted, you're setting up these things and finding somewhere to live. It was crazy.'

Jones faced problems on the pitch as well. As a winger or second striker comfortable taking players on, Neal's tactics didn't quite suit him and Jones didn't feel that he was in a situation to argue his position on the field.

'I wish there had been more of an open-door talking relationship [with Neal],' he admits. 'There wasn't a discussion about what I could do and where I could fit in. I was put on that right side and I was running up and down. I expected to be brought in as more of an attacking player. I found the ball skying over my head quite a bit! I was just running up and down. That's where Phil felt I would fit the best but I don't feel it was my best position, I was better as a winger in a 4-3-3 or as a striker.'

It didn't help that the Sky Blues got off to a rotten start to the season. An opening-day draw with Wimbledon was followed by three defeats, including two 4-0 thrashings. Dublin helped to lift the gloom with a goal on his debut in a 2-2 draw with QPR at the start of September, before Jones came off the bench to win a penalty as City picked up their first win of the season, six matches in, against Leeds. The new signings were quickly making their impact, particularly Dublin.

'I came in playing up front with Peter Ndlovu, Roy Wegerle and Cobi Jones and I formed a relationship with all of them,' he says. 'I was hungry to play, hungry to score goals. I wanted to prove to myself that I could do it after leaving United. If I could prove it to myself then I could prove it to anyone. I just wanted to score goals. I had got myself out of practice because of the injury. I'd been out for eight months at United with a broken leg and a broken ankle. It was frustrating and I knew I wasn't going to get on the pitch at United, so Coventry was the perfect place to be. Phil said he wanted to get this and that player and, lo and behold, we had some incredible players in that squad.'

Dublin notched eight goals for the club by the start of November, while Cobi Jones got his first goal in a 1-0 win over Norwich on 19 November. However, as was often the case with Coventry, inconsistency was to rear its ugly head once more. After a decent enough first three months of the season, a 1-0 away win over West Ham left the club tenth in the table towards the end of November, but a poor run was on the way. Eleven games in the league without a win meant the Sky Blues plummeted into the relegation zone by the start of February. Ahead of a trip to Selhurst Park to face Crystal Palace, talk between fans was that Neal's days were numbered. Despite a 2-0 win, this proved to be the case and he was sacked shortly afterwards. The match was bittersweet for Cobi Jones, a man who had struggled to fit into Neal's team for much of the season.

'This game was the first time Phil Neal played me as a striker,' he says. 'I ended up scoring and I was like, "Finally! I have some freedom to show what I can do." I sprinted the whole distance to the back corner at Palace where our fans were to celebrate with them. I have such great memories that I will never forget of that goal. It was unfortunate that it was the last game for Phil Neal. I finally thought they understood and I had sent the message after getting the opportunity. Then I got mono [glandular fever] and was out. That kind of sealed the deal with me.'

The deal was also very much sealed for Neal. Bryan Richardson had been at the club throughout Neal's reign but had by now become the public face of the board and perhaps a change was needed. Neal had steered the club to a more than creditable 11th the previous year, but Coventry were now in a relegation battle and fans seemed uninspired by the football being played.

Team	P	GD	Pts
16. QPR	26	-6	31
17. Coventry	28	-18	31
18. Crystal Palace	28	-7	30
19. Everton	27	-9	30

'For some reason the fans never took to [Neal],' says Richardson. 'He worked his socks off. We finished 11th under him but for some reason he never caught the imagination. The crowds dropped to about 12,000. It was a hard day to say to Phil that his time was up.'

'Bryan Richardson always said to me that Phil Neal was his best manager because he got the club to its highest position under him,' Jim Brown adds. 'But you always felt Phil wasn't quite the right man. He seemed like a dead man walking almost from day one, despite finishing 11th. There was always a feeling that he wasn't going to last that long. Bryan had big ambitions. He had the support of Geoffrey Robinson and Derek Higgs at this stage – people with money and connections. You could see that there was money in the Premier League. That's when Geoffrey jumped on the bandwagon because he'd never been a Coventry fan before.'

Richardson and Robinson were among a new cast of characters about to take centre stage at Highfield Road. High-profile times were coming and they were kicked into gear by appointing one of the most high-profile characters that Coventry City has ever seen.

4.

The Glitz and Glamour
of Big Ron

AS CITY'S stuttering form continued throughout the 1994/95 season, Phil Neal's time at the club came to an end. The board's choice to replace the former England coach echoed back to Neal's predecessor. No, Bobby Gould wasn't returning for a third stint in charge, but he certainly shared something with the man who was to become a high-profile appointment for the Sky Blues – they were both monumentally huge characters. Perhaps it's just coincidence, but the somewhat dour tenure of Phil Neal is sandwiched between two of the biggest characters to ever step foot into Highfield Road. Before Neal there was the hometown kid, the madcap Gould, and following him came the always-charismatic Big Ron Atkinson. Atkinson had been sacked by Aston Villa in November 1994, a decision that still puzzles him. Nevertheless, it helped to pave the way for Ron's arrival at Highfield Road.

'I'd left the Villa, which quite frankly was a bit of a joke, and the Coventry chairman and vice-chairman came to see me,' Ron recalls. 'I'd been lined up for the Tottenham job at the time and I thought Coventry was local and I knew the area and people there. I'd always seen it as a very friendly club. I thought I'd been in Madrid, Sheffield and I didn't want to uproot again.'

Ron's arrival in the dugout instantly did the trick, getting 4,000 extra fans through the gates for his home debut against West Ham. Myself and my dad were there that day and we, along with the other 17,500 fans inside Highfield Road, were treated to a 2-0 win, with Peter Ndlovu and Mike Marsh combining with a goal and an assist apiece.

'From day one Ron got the crowd going,' club historian Jim Brown says. 'Gates in that season had been very poor. From day one Ron got the attendances up and got the team playing attractive football. People started talking about the team again.'

Chairman Bryan Richardson reveals that it was in Ron's interest to make sure the crowds flooded into Highfield Road.

'I called [Ron] our Pied Piper,' he says. 'He rattled the people of Coventry into coming to support us. In his first game, instead of 12,000 we had 18,000. The key to that was in Ron's contract I put a clause that he got, I think it was £5 a head, for attendances over 12,000 people. That made him sing for his supper. It did the trick.'

Adding thousands to the gate wasn't Ron's only impact; he certainly made an impression on the squad that he inherited.

'He introduced himself and said there was someone in that room who would surprise him because he wouldn't have realised how good they actually were,' remembers Jonathan Gould. 'All of us sat there and thought, "Yeah, that's me!"'

Midfielder Willie Boland suggests that the Big Ron who arrived at Ryton to take his first training session was exactly the Big Ron that we had all seen in the media throughout his high-profile career.

'Ron had come into the club and he is what he portrays himself to be,' Boland says. 'He's this larger-than-life character. He came on to the training pitch with his tan and his shorts, socks and football boots. He'd join in with the five-a-sides, even though I think to be honest with you his best days were behind him! He still got involved. He was a

WHEN THE SKY WAS BLUE

good guy to have around. Having him come in gave everyone a lift straightaway. He also had a lot of contacts in the game and he tried getting people into the club.'

One player who was right at the top of Ron's shopping list was defender David Burrows. He had worked with the left-back at West Brom years earlier and, for a team more accustomed to signing lower-league talents, agreeing a deal for a man who had won a league title with Liverpool just a few seasons earlier marked a change in recruitment approach. The transfer fee too, at just a shade over £1m, while not earth shattering, was a step up from what Neal, Gould and co. had been allocated for defensive reinforcements in the years before.

'I knew Ron from West Brom and liked him,' Burrows says. 'I had no hesitation whatsoever coming to Coventry. I would have gone to whatever club Ron was at if he had wanted me. I spoke to Ron when he was at Villa and he didn't have the money to buy me from West Ham, and he said to sit tight. In the meantime, he was sacked and then got in touch to say there was a chance of him taking over at Coventry and would I be interested in signing. Of course I was interested, it was taking me back to the Midlands and working with Ron again.'

Burrows adds that it wasn't merely familiarity that enticed him to Coventry. Instead, he, and several other players, were attracted by the exciting times that Atkinson's arrival was seemingly ushering in for the club.

'Ron was pivotal in these players coming to Coventry,' Burrows asserts. 'No disrespect to Coventry, but they could never compete on the finance side of it. It was a really well-run club and it had to be because if anything went wrong it would be financially disastrous for them. Ron going there gave them a chance of doing more than battling in that bottom six. He attracted higher-profile players. Players didn't go to Coventry for money. Most of the players I've spoken to took a pay cut to play for Ron at Coventry and that says all you need to know about Ron. Straightaway I felt a warmth at the club. It was the best five years of my career.'

Atkinson also oversaw changes in the way that the media was treated at the club. Amid an influx of interest from journalists up and down the country, he courted local and national reporters in textbook Big Ron style.

'I think Phil Neal would see himself being as big of a character in football as Ron but to everybody else it was all of a sudden here is the big man, larger than life in a similar way to how Snoz had been,' recalls Stuart Linnell. 'He had this bit of romantic pizazz about him because of what he had done previously. The transformation at the club was huge. The national media was suddenly all over the club, coming to matches they never previously would have. At the post-match press conferences loads of us would go into Ron's room, where he would hold court. He had this huge stainless steel bowl on his desk full of seafood. The idea was you would dip in, get a shrimp or whatever it was, have some of that and there was always pink champagne around. It was that kind of aura around the place. He brought an interest to the club that we hadn't had before.'

But, while interest and investment in the club was certainly on the up, Atkinson was still working to a comparatively lower budget than he had been used to with the likes of Manchester United and Aston Villa. A degree of wheeling and dealing was required and, as well as the aforementioned Burrows, Atkinson also quickly brought in veteran midfielder Kevin Richardson, who had been his captain at the Villa, for £300,000. Straightaway, there certainly was a lift on the pitch. Back-to-back wins, against West Ham and Leicester, began an unbeaten six-match run. The 4-2 win over Leicester, for whom relegation already looked a foregone conclusion, lifted the Sky Blues to 12th. With three wins in a row, one under Phil Neal and two with Big Ron, the club had shunted from the relegation zone to just one point behind Aston Villa and the top half of the Premier League. The momentum was slowed slightly by the pair of 0-0 draws that followed, the first against Southampton and then away to Aston Villa. Despite only having been in the hot seat for a matter of weeks, the latter match saw Atkinson pulling the strings with the media in a way that only he could.

'In one of my early games we played Villa in a night match,' he says. 'Sky were supposed to be at Anfield but it got called off for some reason. I rang the guy at Sky because they were paying quite a bit of money to be televised. I said, "Get to Villa Park, I'm going back there, there will be a bit of emotion, you can put your camera on the bus, you can do this and that." The money was terrific for the club. We should have beaten them. Nuddy missed a chance he would normally slot away in the last kick of the match.'

While Ndlovu may have been guilty of a late miss against the Villa, he more than made up for his sloppiness in front of goal 12 days later as the Sky Blues faced Liverpool. Sandwiched between those matches, however, was a home fixture with soon-to-be champions Blackburn Rovers. Coventry put in what Atkinson described afterwards as the best 45 minutes since he had been at the club in a superb first-half display. Hesitant defending from Ian Pearce allowed Dublin to sneak in and scuff the ball past Tim Flowers to put City ahead at the break. Unfortunately, this was the proverbial game of two halves. Rovers came out, as you would expect for a team looking to pull away at the top of the table, all guns blazing, and peppered Jonathan Gould's goal with shots. With just three minutes left, Gould misjudged a Graham Le Saux ball into the box and Shearer managed to outjump the Sky Blues keeper and head in an equaliser. We were sitting behind Gould's goal that afternoon and couldn't believe that Shearer had managed to get up above him. It was like Maradona vs Shilton in 1986. But without the handball. And with slightly less at stake.

It was a goal that provided a source of embarrassment for Gould and one of his defenders.

'I remember saying to Alan Shearer a few minutes from the end, "It's not your day today,"' Brian Borrows recalls. 'Then, a minute later he got above Jonathan Gould and headed one in. I wished I hadn't said anything!'

Still, a point against the team at the top of the table was nothing to cry about. Next, it was on to that match with Liverpool. The Sky Blues travelled to Anfield in 12th place, level with Chelsea and Arsenal in 11th and 10th, respectively, a point ahead of the Villa and enjoying a comfortable eight-point cushion over the relegation places. Their hosts were fourth, but this Graeme Souness team weren't the force that they once were, having already lost ten matches that season. That was soon to be 11 and it was pretty much solely down to the magic of Ndlovu. He gave City the lead by driving a back-post shot past David James after 21 minutes. Less than a quarter of an hour later he doubled City's advantage from the penalty spot after James had felled former Liverpool man Mike Marsh in the box. What looked like an incredibly soft penalty, for a tug on Robbie Fowler's shirt by Brian Borrows, allowed Liverpool to halve the deficit, but Ndlovu's best was still to come. A run straight through the middle of the park bamboozled the lumbering Neil Ruddock and Nuddy fired into the bottom corner to become the first visiting player to notch a hat-trick at Anfield for 34 years. A late David Burrows own goal pulled the score back to 3-2 but that's how it ended, as City secured a scintillating win.

'That was a really sweet victory,' Burrows recalls. 'I left Liverpool in 1993 and hadn't settled since. I hadn't got Liverpool out of my system. On the night we absorbed a lot of pressure and Nuddy came through with a hat-trick. That was the decline of Graeme Souness's Liverpool. It was a shock result to most people but we deserved that victory. Peter was Ron's dream. Ron loved a player like Peter, someone who was carefree. You had Peter Ndlovu in the team because he was going to give you something nobody else would.'

'That was the highlight of my career,' Ndlovu adds. 'For me, just a mere African boy who had come to look for work in England to score three at Anfield, that was very special. That will forever stick out on my CV and in my life as a number-one achievement. The only thing people questioned was I scored three goals but I had supported Liverpool for my entire life! But I was working for Coventry and I had to do what I had to do.'

Team	P	GD	Pts
7. Tottenham	31	+9	48
8. Sheffield Wednesday	34	-2	43
9. Coventry	34	-13	43
10. Wimbledon	32	-17	42

Jim Brown has seen the great and good of Coventry City in his decades as a fan, and the magnitude of this particular result isn't lost on him.

'To win at Anfield was just incredible,' he beams. 'That game was all about Peter Ndlovu. But then we slipped back and had to get our skates on to stay up.'

Slip back we most certainly did. A bruising 3-0 defeat to Leeds brought City back down to earth with a bump four days later, but that wasn't the biggest event to come out of Elland Road that week. Instead, that was when Gordon Strachan moved on a free from Leeds to Coventry. He was billed as assistant manager and, in an unusual move, was slated to succeed Atkinson as manager in the following years.

'I signed Strachan at Man U when Alex [Ferguson] said he was finished. He was 27 at the time,' Atkinson says, picking up the story of how he helped attract Strachan to the club. 'He was the best right-sided midfielder who played for me. I'd put him in my top five players of all time for me.

Then he went to Leeds. I tried desperately to take him to Sheffield Wednesday but I think Howard Wilkinson made him the highest-paid player in the country. Part of my brief when I went to Coventry was to pick and groom somebody to take over as manager in a year or two. Ray Wilkins was one that I identified and then I asked if Strach fancied it and he came down as an assistant manager. He would sit in the board meetings. I told him to just come in and listen because it was a totally different world to being a player. He was learning on the job. You very seldom get that opportunity. I used to involve him on contract details with players, just sitting in the office as we were doing them. You'll all have your own way but he could at least learn certain things from that.'

Bryan Richardson recalls that he and Atkinson were of the same mind on the decision to bring in Strachan.

'When Ron joined I said to him he would probably only do two or three years at the most so let's get someone to come in and learn from him and do a lot of the training, because Ron wasn't going to do a lot of the training ground stuff, so we needed a first-team coach,' he says. 'I was at Ron's house and he asked who I fancied. I said I would put two names down on a piece of paper and he would write two names and then we'd swap pieces of paper. We both wrote down the same two names, one of which was Gordon.'

'I retired from first-team football at Leeds,' adds Strachan. 'Howard [Wilkinson] felt I wasn't the influence I was before, which is understandable. My last game was against Liverpool, a 0-0. We sat on the Monday and decided it was time to call it a day. We agreed I would look after the reserve team. That gave me the bug for coaching. I loved it. Ron Atkinson asked me if I'd like to come to Coventry to be assistant manager. I said yeah and we agreed between Bryan Richardson, Ron and myself that when Ron stopped managing Coventry I would take over. That gave me a clear pathway. I could learn under Ron and it seemed like a good pathway.'

The pathway, however, could have been a slippery slope down to Division One.

Atkinson's initial magic showed its first signs of having worn off as City followed that 3-0 defeat against Leeds with a 1-0 reverse against QPR. Coventry were back looking over their shoulder again, and while they were six points above the relegation zone, many teams below had multiple matches in hand and superior goal difference. If they were to avoid being sucked back into a dogfight, City needed a lift. Luckily, they had one of the finest midfielders of his generation in their midst.

'[Gordon] came down and we'd have little training games and five-a-sides and I'm watching him and I called him in one day and said, "You know what? You're the best player we've got!"' Atkinson laughs. 'I told him he was better than any of the others.'

'When I got there, Ron had me joining in training and he realised that I could still play!' says Strachan of his decision to get his boots back out. 'The more I look back the more I think the big guy conned me, getting me in thinking I was assistant but getting me playing again. He was telling me how good I was and that I should still be playing. I ended up playing again.'

While undoubtedly a class act in midfield, Strachan couldn't do it on his own and, after a win against Sheffield Wednesday, City slipped to three defeats in a row. Incredibly, the Sky Blues had shot up to ninth in the table after the Ndlovu-inspired win over Liverpool but five defeats in the next six matches after that famous night at Anfield saw City staring in the face of a relegation battle. This left them 18th in the table, just a point above the relegation trap door, an opening made wider that season as four teams rather than the usual three would drop out of the division. The final of those six matches, a 2-0 defeat against bottom-of-the-table Ipswich, looked to be a hammer blow.

Team	P	GD	Pts
16. West Ham	40	-7	46
17. Everton	40	-8	46
18. Coventry	40	-20	46
19. Crystal Palace	40	-12	45

Atkinson needed a plan. Thankfully, he had a pair of aces up his sleeve. The first card he played was to pull in a few favours for an unconventional piece of pre-match preparation.

'I came back into the team against Tottenham,' says Julian Darby, who returned to the midfield for the must-win match, his first appearance since Phil Neal's sacking. 'We were desperate for a win. Everyone thought we would go to Ipswich and win and we got beat so we had to win against Tottenham. I got pulled and was told that I was playing. With Ron's connections we trained at Rod Stewart's house. Rod had this house in, I think it was Epping Forest, and he had a football pitch at the bottom of his garden. We trained there on the morning of the game. That seemed to take away some of the pressure because you arrived on the bus and you were at Rod Stewart's house! It was unbelievable and it helped people forget about the pressure of the game.'

As if that wasn't enough, Atkinson also had his veteran player-assistant tuned up and ready to go. The 38-year-old Strachan lined up in midfield against Spurs at White Hart Lane in the penultimate match of the 1994/95 season. Cajoling the Scot out of semi-retirement for this run of matches may have seemed like a desperate move; however, it quickly became apparent to all inside White Hart Lane that night that it was an absolute masterstroke. Strachan tore Spurs apart, having a hand in all three goals in a 3-1 win. The opener came when Strachan cut out a pass just outside his own box. He drove down the majority of the pitch before laying the ball off to Roy Wegerle on his right. The American then spotted that the flame-haired coach had overlapped on the outside and played the ball out to him. Strachan's cross was met at the far post with a diving Ndlovu header. The gamble was paying off already. The rewards kept on coming and Ndlovu was again the benefactor just after the hour mark. Strachan skipped down the right-hand side, showing Justin Edinburgh, a full-back 13 years his junior, a clean pair of heels before being hacked down in the box by the Spurs defender. Ndlovu converted the resulting spot kick. Five minutes later, a delicious one-two between that man Strachan and Darby resulted in Dublin firing home from close range. City were 3-0 up and blasting away any relegation fears. Darren Anderton bagged a late consolation goal but this was to be Strachan's night as he helped guarantee survival with a fine 3-1 win.

'We went to Tottenham and he tore them to pieces,' Atkinson says. 'Justin Edinburgh wrote an article saying Strachan was the most difficult opponent he'd ever played against. We beat them 3-1 at White Hart Lane when they had all the Klinsmanns and Sheringhams and Andertons, and that meant we were safe – we didn't even have to go to the last game of the season! Gordon that night, it was like having a young George Best in your team. He picked his games from there but he went in from time to time and did the job.'

Strachan himself recalls that it wasn't just the boss and his team-mates that were impressed by his performance. There was a German World Cup winner waiting for him in the dressing room afterwards.

'I enjoyed that game and I felt like an influence again,' Strachan says. 'It wasn't easy playing at that age, though. After the game, Jurgen Klinsmann came into the dressing room and asked if we could swap strips. I said, "Oh yeah, very good, smashing."'

Strachan, quite rightly, took a heap of plaudits for his performance, but Ndlovu once again more than played his part. It wasn't just his two goals that stood out – he also gave a future Premier League winner a torrid time.

'The game at White Hart Lane had Strachan running it,' recalls Jim Brown. 'The other thing that night was Peter Ndlovu was up against Sol Campbell at right-back. Ndlovu destroyed him so much that Campbell was substituted in the first half. Ndlovu was just unplayable in those days.'

The win meant that City went into the final day, and their Highfield Road match against Everton, with safety already assured.

Team	P	GD	Pts
16. Coventry	41	-18	49
17. Sheffield Wednesday	41	-11	48
18. Aston Villa	41	-5	47
19. Crystal Palace	41	-14	45

David Burrows certainly wasn't surprised by the positive impact that Atkinson, at least initially, had on the club's fortunes. He reveals that the secret was through Big Ron doing what Big Ron does. Not one for toiling over tactics, he instead put a smile on faces and used his personable nature to get the best out of his squad.

'Ron had this knack of getting the best out of players and that wasn't through filling them with technical and tactical stuff during the week,' Burrows says. 'Ron wanted his players to work hard but he wanted them to work hard when they were playing football, not just running around. He wanted his footballers to play. Every day he wanted a five-a-side, whether we were doing shape or whatever, he wanted to finish the day with a competitive match. He wasn't a big coach or tactical man, he was someone who played players in the right positions, got them fit and wanted them to enjoy themselves. He wanted his players to express themselves. He wanted young players to not be frightened about coming into the first team. He would tell us we were as good as anybody. He put so much confidence into me and he was one of the best motivators in sport. Ron got Gordon to come to the club. That gave everybody a boost. He was a winner and a genuine football nut. He came in with his enthusiasm. Gordon gave the club a boost when we could have easily gone down.'

Jonathan Gould benefited from an injury to Ogrizovic to play in seven of the final 12 matches of the season. He concurs that the Atkinson–Strachan partnership was pivotal in securing safety for the Sky Blues that season.

'We needed someone of the ilk of Big Ron to come in and give us that bounce,' the goalkeeper adds. 'If he hadn't come in I'm convinced we would have got relegated that year. Ron came in and saved us from the drop but Gordon was a big part of that. Gordon at 38 was the fittest in the group. He was the most enthusiastic. He was off his head sometimes but that's because he was a winner and he came in and his destiny was to ensure we didn't get relegated. It was his survival instinct because he had been brought in as an experienced player, but I'm sure Gordon also saw it as his pathway into management.'

Gordon Strachan certainly was on a pathway to management and, as the 1994/95 season ended, there was cause of optimism that the following year would be one in which fans could look up the table rather than down. Atkinson and Strachan had steadied the ship and secured survival. Meaningful investment on the pitch seemed to be coming to fruition with a host of signings lined up for that summer, and there was a feel-good factor, the likes of which hadn't been seen since Bobby Gould's team took the Premier League by storm early on in the 1992/93 and 1993/94 seasons. The last thing any of us expected, however, was that the 1995/96 season would go down to a final-day battle against the drop.

5.

Here Comes the Money

FOR MANY, 1995/96 is the year that Coventry really changed approach. The days of trawling the lower leagues for bargains were gone. In its place was Big Ron attracting genuine Premier League talent, aided by a significant loosening of the club's purse strings. While the net spend may have been, by today's standards, a relatively modest sum at just under £4m, it represented a new way of thinking from the board. Buoyed no doubt by Big Ron putting bums on seats, Coventry were ready to finally back a manager in the transfer market. Bobby Gould and his little black book seemed a lifetime away as Big Ron started splashing the cash. Of course, Coventry weren't the only club to be spending the Premier League's new-found riches. Across the league, transfer spending was up. Particularly eye-catching moves that close-season included Dennis Bergkamp and David Platt joining Arsenal for combined fees well in excess of £10m and Newcastle paying £6m to QPR for Les Ferdinand.

Ahead of the season's kick-off, several big-name signings came into Highfield Road, including Isaias, a £500,000 buy, who became the first Brazilian to play in the Premier League. For me, this was the summer signing that caused the most excitement. I was just shy of my tenth birthday so perhaps my judgement wasn't the greatest, but the prospect of a Brazilian playing in the middle of the park for my beloved Sky Blues was mouth-watering. A legend back in Portugal, he caught the eye early on, particularly in a 2-2 draw at Stamford Bridge, with his masterful range of passing and penchant for a screamer. Unfortunately, he was one who burned brightly but faded disappointingly quickly.

'What a player he was,' says Atkinson. 'I'd seen him play for Benfica and absolutely murder Arsenal one night at Highbury. He ripped them apart. Somebody said we could get him. I kept flashing back to that match. He was great in training. I remember us playing Chelsea one night and Ruud Gullit was playing for Chelsea. We drew two each and as we came off there was a journalist called Brian Glanville and he said in the press conference that Isaias was the best foreign signing any English club had ever made. I always remembered that. He was a terrific player with a thunderbolt of a shot. Maybe we didn't use him in the best way. We had to have Ndlovu, Dion and Whelan in the team, so we couldn't really pack the midfield. Nowadays you might pack the midfield and have an insurance man in the middle, and Isaias would have been great. We went on a pre-season tour in Portugal and he was like a god. The fans and players loved him. He wasn't quite Ronaldo but he was certainly up with the gods. He'd be great in the current Man City team; he wouldn't half look a player.'

'We didn't realise that he was a legend in Portugal!' adds David Burrows. 'He'd come from Benfica and was a big name. I went on holiday in Portugal and everyone was asking, "How is Isaias? Our hero!" He had injuries and didn't see eye to eye at all with Gordon.'

Also signed that summer were two who would hang around for a little longer than the enigmatic Brazilian. In fact, this pair would go on to become City stalwarts, and big favourites of Gordon Strachan. The duo in question were Paul Telfer and Paul Williams.

'We played against [Telfer] when he was with Luton and I was at Villa and he impressed me with his work rate and his ability in the air,' Ron continues. 'He was exceptional in the air and he gave good service to the club. I had Sean Flynn on the right-hand side and he was decent, but I swapped him for big Paul Williams from Derby, who could do a spell in midfield or at the back.'

There was also a clear-out of several players that hung over from the Bobby Gould and Phil Neal days, with the likes of Julian Darby, Leigh Jenkinson, Paul Williams (no, not that Paul Williams, the other one!) and John Williams all moving on during the season. I remember being particularly upset by the aforementioned departure of Flynn, not least because I'd had his name on the back of my 1994/95 away shirt. I also thought he did a good job in a variety of positions and popped up with his share of goals. Still, in Big Ron we trust was the mantra of the summer.

One of the most audacious pieces of potential business – but one that showed that the purse strings still remained somewhat tightened despite the rise in spending – was an attempt to sign Wolves legend Steve Bull. Atkinson was keen and the deal seemed on until Bull backed out and decided to stay put. Many years later, Bull told the *Quickly Kevin, Will He Score?* podcast that a deal was on the table with Coventry to earn the same money that he would bring in at Wolves. Unfortunately, it would take him five years to earn the money at the Sky Blues rather than three at Molineux! Suffice to say, Bull decided that the grass wasn't greener on the other side.

One marquee name who did sign was John Salako. The Crystal Palace winger had picked up five caps for England and, despite his injury problems, remained a big name for the Sky Blues to attract. Salako, however, reveals that he very nearly joined up with title-chasing Newcastle United instead.

'Kevin Keegan gave me a ring in the summer when I'd just gone on holiday,' Salako says. 'He told me to fly back and sign for Newcastle, so I flew back and headed up there. It was the beginning of the end for Kevin because he was in one camp with Douglas Hall and then there was Sir John Hall and the other side. They wanted to sign Ginola. He was asking for a lot of money and Kevin said he wasn't paying that money and he would get me instead. I was a pawn in a game of chess really. I was like, "Why don't you sign both of us?!" They ended up signing Ginola so I came back. Then my agent said Ron Atkinson wanted me at Cov. I thought that sounded great. I spoke to Ron and jumped at it. Ron was very charismatic, he was a leader. He sold his plan to me and that he wanted to take the club to the next level and push on. It sounded exciting. I'd always admired Coventry, it was a lovely part of the country and I was excited to join.'

That summer, Ron, alongside Gordon, took his first pre-season with the club. Ron, renowned for his carefree spirit and emphasis on work with the ball, and Gordon, a wily competitor who was to put far more stock into fitness, seemed unlikely bedfellows.

'Ron was an old-style manager, a great motivator, loved joining in with training,' says Jim Brown. 'Gordon was a much more serious character. He wanted to do things properly. You felt the club was going places with those two there.'

There was a noticeable difference between the two for the players as well. Veteran defender Brian Borrows, who Ron had tried to sign during his time at Villa, noted that the pair weren't quite always on the same page when it came to training.

'Ron's strength was his man-management,' he says. 'Gordon was more tactical and the fitness side. At times you could see Gordon was probably a bit frustrated when Ron would wander out with his cup of tea and say, "Come on, let's get the five-a-side goals out." You'd see Gordon's face drop because he thought we were going to do X, Y and Z. Ron would join in and pretend he was Ginola or someone else. They were chalk and cheese.'

Well, they do say that opposites attract, and Dave Busst was another who was impressed by the managerial set-up. The defender had been injured when Atkinson arrived but would go on to make 17 league appearances in 1995/96.

'Ron and Gordon were really good together,' he says. 'Gordon came in and had all of the energy and worked on the technical side and Ron was a great man-manager. Ron wanted the team spirit, he protected us in front of the camera and absolutely hammered us on the training ground. That's what you want as a player, you don't want the manager digging you out in public.'

Atkinson carried with him a famed reputation for building a strong team spirit wherever he went. Busst reveals that this was certainly the case at Coventry.

'He wanted us to socialise,' he adds. 'There wasn't a drinking culture but it was encouraged that on our day off we socialised together and we did. He wanted us to go away at the end of the season as well, and he came with us! We thrived on the way he treated us. Yes, he absolutely hammered us when things weren't going right but we loved training. We would always have a five-a-side and he was involved in the Champions League, so whoever the star man that week was, that was who Ron would be in training. You'd curse if he was on your side because you knew you'd be doing the forfeit because you'd have Ron standing up front pretending to be Del Piero. If you were on Ron's side that meant Gordon was on the other side as well, and that didn't quite add up!'

Atkinson and Strachan may have had slightly different approaches to the training ground five-a-sides, but Ron suggests the pair had no issues working together and ironing out their pre-season plans.

'We would just pool ideas on what we wanted to work on each day,' he says regarding the duo's approach to pre-season. 'Early on would have been a strong emphasis on running but I always liked training with the ball. Give them the physical stuff for a couple of days and then get the balls out. We worked hard though. I used to call it a burst on the banjo, giving them half an hour of really battling. When I played, we would train twice a day in pre-season. But I found if you worked hard in the morning you'd come back in the afternoon stiff. I worked them hard in the mornings. I used to speak to Bill Shankly a lot and that's what he did at Liverpool. I never wanted a football club to be a prisoner-of-war camp. Someone once told me that enthusiasm is free. I wanted people who were enthusiastic and keen.'

The enthusiasm of even the chirpiest of players would be tested by what was to come. An opening-day thrashing at the hands of Newcastle set the tone for what was to be a poor start to the campaign. Despite having upped the spending, City were still short on quality and in need of further reinforcements. Richard Shaw joined John Salako in jumping ship from recently relegated Crystal Palace and arrived at Highfield Road. Shaw is honest about exactly what, or who, attracted him to the club.

'Having Ron Atkinson at the helm and Gordon Strachan being there as well helped a lot,' he says. 'I'd just got into the England squad in 1995. Palace had been relegated and I really needed to stay in the Premier League to have a chance of staying in the squad. I got a call saying Coventry were interested. I spoke to John Salako and he said it was a good place to come and he could see what Big Ron was trying to do. I didn't think I'd be there for ten years, I have to say. But anyone who has met Ron will know the charisma he has and the presence. Strachs was there as well as a fantastic coach. It was a good fit. As soon as I met Ron he sold it to me.'

The reinforcements had arrived, but City's early season form remained a cause for concern. A run of three losses in a row in September, including 5-1 and 3-0 hammerings at the hands of Blackburn and Aston Villa, respectively, wasn't what we had in mind for this season; this season was supposed to be different. A point was gained in a 0-0 draw with Liverpool, a match so dull that it was given 13 seconds of airtime on *Match of the Day* and, in lieu of the usual voiceover from Gerald Sinstadt or Ray Stubbs, instead just featured a graphic at the bottom of the screen that read 'No goals at Anfield'. Four defeats in the next five took City to one of the most memorable matches of the season, a home fixture with Wimbledon. It wasn't memorable for a thumping win or for the quality of the football on show. Instead, it will do down in the history books, much like a trip to Fratton Park years later, as the Sky Blues came from behind to earn a point in a 3-3 draw. That's impressive enough, but what made it remarkable was that City did it with just nine men after red cards for Paul Williams and Richard Shaw. Salako reckons that it was a result born out of the characters in that Coventry dressing room.

'There was incredible character in the squad,' he says. 'Games like that come down to the desire and character of the players and we would fight for each other. We had great characters and top players as well. There wasn't a moment with that squad where you were allowed to just give up. You had players like Richardson, Ogrizovic, Borrows, who would look at you and tell you that you had to dig in. That was instilled in those players and that dressing room. That result epitomises that team.'

Team	P	GD	Pts
18. QPR	15	-12	11
19. Coventry	15	-18	9
20. Bolton	15	-16	8

While City's early season form was certainly a cause for concern, one bright spark was the goalscoring touch of Dion Dublin. Highlights included a long-range header against Nottingham Forest, not quite Gus Hamer range but still pretty impressive, and a neat spin and finish against Spurs.

The striker hit double figures before Christmas rolled around. This did, however, include the unfortunate incident of bagging a hat-trick against Sheffield Wednesday – only to end up on the wrong end of a 4-3 defeat. Dion's rich vein of goalscoring form was no surprise to Atkinson, who had long admired the frontman.

'I remember when I was at Sheffield Wednesday, we played Cambridge in the cup and Dion put us to the sword that day,' Ron recalls. 'When I was at the Villa we had a few looks at him and nearly took him before Man United came in. We looked at him a lot. I sent Andy Gray to watch him quite a bit.'

'We had Dion Dublin, who was a great captain, professional and a leader,' Richard Shaw adds. 'He brought the changing room together. I'd played against Dion many times when I was at Palace and I thought he was a good player, good in the air and a good hold-up player. But then when you train with him you realise his first touch was unbelievable and so was his movement to buy five yards. In the air he was as good as anybody in the Premier League at the time. It doesn't half make your life easy when you're clipping balls into Dion and you know his first touch is going to stick and he would bring people into play. He just gelled the club together. He made sure new signings were okay. He did all this work behind the scenes. A lot of the camaraderie, a lot of that was down to Dion.'

While Dion was firing and Shaw was certainly a welcome addition, and one who would quickly form a long-lasting partnership with Paul Williams at the heart of defence, Ron was keen to add further quality to the squad. The league position remained dire. The club had notched up just one win, and nine points, from the opening 16 matches. That left Coventry rooted to the foot of the table and Atkinson knew he needed to improve the back line. However, he was realistic about what he could afford when it came to bolstering the squad in the run-up to Christmas.

'I knew I was working in a limited financial market,' he says. 'That wasn't anything new to me. I was looking around the bargain basement. As it developed, what happened out of the blue, I was shopping in the bargain basement and I'd agreed a deal to sign the centre-half Andy Linighan for £300,000. That was the market we were working in and then all of a sudden the chairman asked if I had £3m who would I buy. I wondered what he was talking about. I said of the available players the one would be Chris Coleman from Crystal Palace. He'd played with Richard Shaw, who we'd taken, he was an experienced defender and in that market we weren't going to get someone absolutely top level like a Mark Wright or somebody, but I thought Coleman would work.'

It looked like a deal for Coleman was about to be done, but then City went and spoiled it all by battering the reigning Premier League champions 5-0.

'It's funny how things turn out against you because I had a meeting with Chris Coleman in Oxford on the Friday and we more or less agreed everything,' Ron continues. 'It was the days where you needed to sign 48 hours before a game and we played Blackburn on the Saturday so he said he would go and think about it but everything seemed right. He came to watch us play Blackburn and we beat them 5-0. If we'd have beaten them 1-0, Chris Coleman would have signed for Coventry. Because we beat them 5-0, [Blackburn manager] Ray Harford went, "I need centre-halves," and he went and offered Coleman more. He bought him because we beat them by five.'

One defender who was in the City line-up that day against Blackburn was Chris Whyte. The club had taken the centre-half on loan from the Barry Fry-led Birmingham and he slotted comfortably into the team. Ron was impressed by the new signing, but there was a sting in the tail from Fry.

'I've always had a great relationship with Barry Fry,' Ron says. 'I took Whyte on loan for a month and he was outstanding. I played three at the back that day and he was outstanding. I thought, "I like this." I really liked him in that three. Afterwards we were talking and I told him that was how we would play for the month he was here and, who knows, he might end up here permanently. He said, "I can't, I'm suspended for the next three weeks!" I phoned Barry and said he'd done me and he said it was about time he won one!'

While Ron may have lost out to Barry Fry on that particular deal, John Salako suggests that giving out such a hiding was a testament to the confidence that the manager had inspired in his players.

'There was so much belief in that squad,' he says. 'On our day, we were a fantastic side. That Blackburn game was great for the fans. The Cov fans were great. They weren't moaning and over the top when things didn't go right. They believed in the team. They were always there backing the side. Ron was great at building the belief in the squad. We'd have a team meeting, say before a game against Liverpool, and Ron would read out the team and he'd say, "McManaman, Redknapp, Fowler, I wouldn't swap any of them for you guys, I love you guys, you guys are as good as them." When you looked around the dressing room and saw Noel Whelan, Huckerby, Ndlovu, you were like, "Yeah, we're not bad!"'

While capable of beating anyone on our day, there was a concern that at this point clubs were beginning to plough huge money in for transfers and wages. Despite upping their game by splashing a few million, Coventry were still in danger of being left behind. Behind the scenes, new ways of getting money into the club were being trialled. One such way was what has been dubbed the 'buy a player' scheme. This saw benefactors put up cash for transfers.

'[Buy a player] wasn't as it sounded,' Bryan Richardson contests. 'It was a way of getting around the rules of outside investors putting money up for players. The theory of it, which passed the rules at the time and still would today, I assume, was that if, for instance, Noel Whelan was bought for £2m and the theory was, if and when we sold him, the first £2m would go back to the investor and the profit would stay with the club. Of course, it was never the intention that the money from the first situation would ever happen. In other words, there were two investors only – Geoffrey Robinson and Derek Higgs. There was no interest on the money for two years and then it was just bank interest rather than commercial rate interest. It was a good deal for the club.'

Long-time club secretary Graham Hover distinctly recalls his first encounter with one of these benefactors – Labour MP Robinson.

'My earliest memory of Geoffrey was him calling me up and saying he wanted to come for a chat,' Hover says. 'He came in and his opening line was, "I want to buy the club." I told him I wasn't sure it was actually for sale. It didn't take long after that for us to get him involved. Bryan could see the wealth and recognised that he could use that money to bring in better-quality players. Geoffrey was always going to be in the club from then. Bryan was a businessman and was very good at using other people's money.'

The aforementioned Whelan came in from his boyhood club Leeds just before Christmas 1995 and made an instant impact. He netted three goals in three matches over the Christmas period.

'I got a call while I was in bed on a Sunday morning,' Whelan explains. 'It was Howard Wilkinson asking me to go into the club. I knew what was happening without asking him. I went in and spoke to Howard. He apologised and said they had turned down two offers prior to Coventry's offer. They were trying to get other players off the books so they could keep me but these more experienced players were sticking to their guns with their contracts. Leeds had no option but to sell me because they needed the money. It was a difficult day. Leeds were the biggest club in the world to me. I walked out in tears.'

Despite the emotional farewell, Whelan hit the ground running at his new club and made an immediate impression on all around him.

'Noel Whelan was one I thought was destined to go to the very top,' Atkinson laments. 'I would have hung my hat on him going to the very top. He could have been an England player. Gordon and I disagreed on Noel because Gordon saw he had great energy and playing in midfield better suited him. I preferred him playing against the last defender because he could shift the ball on people. I could see him becoming a big goalscorer. When he was centre-forward playing on the last man, he was terrific.'

After one win in the first 16, the Sky Blues now hit a run of just two defeats in 13 as they eased away from the drop zone. The club matched their points tally of nine from those first 16 matches in the next four, pushing them out of the relegation zone by the end of 1995. Whelan was at the heart of the club's upturn in fortunes. His shimmy and finish proved the difference in a 2-1 win over Everton two days before Christmas. A week later, a delicious turn and shot helped City to another 2-1 victory, this time against Bolton. Perhaps the finest of many fine goals from his career came on New Year's Day as he seemingly side-stepped the entire Southampton starting 11 as he ended a mazy run with a prodded finish past the keeper to earn Coventry a draw. All these years later, I still see Whelan's trademark as the dinked finish over an oncoming goalkeeper, and in looking back for this book I see that this comes from two goals within a week of each other. The first was a delicate chip over David Seaman in a 1-1 draw at Highbury, while the latter was a carbon copy at Highfield Road to earn a win over Chelsea and give Whelan his seventh goal in 11 matches.

'I had an intelligence about the game of when to make a run, when to play a pass and what to do when I was in on goal,' Whelan says of the rich form he found himself in. 'That doesn't make me better than other players but it makes me a little bit different, that I could do certain things with the ball that others couldn't do. When I was in on goal I generally wouldn't miss. Inside the box, outside the box, volleys, I felt I could tick most boxes and keep calm and composed in front of goal.'

There was more transfer activity around this time as defender Liam Daish and attacker Eoin Jess joined for £1.5m and £2m, respectively, within a fortnight of each other in February. Atkinson describes Daish as 'just what Coventry needed – a solid scrapper who would battle and stick his head in'.

'There was a buzz around the club when I joined,' Daish says of his move. 'Big Ron had come in, so had Gordon Strachan, and they had players like Dion Dublin, John Salako and Noel Whelan. There was a feeling that the club didn't just want to survive, they wanted to push on and achieve. They were trying to mix it with the big lads.'

Daish's addition to the squad, however, did mean yet another centre-half entering the fray. Healthy competition is one thing, but it may have been a case of too many cooks.

'Ron was at Aston Villa and Manchester United with unbelievable squads,' says Richard Shaw. 'We weren't that at the time and we needed a bit of coaching and to gel with our roles and different partners. I played alongside David Rennie, Dave Busst, Liam Daish, Paul Williams, Dion played at centre-half at times, Chris Whyte came in on loan. There was an uncertainty at times, there was never a stable back four. We worked a lot that year and I think you saw the benefits of that the year after.'

As Shaw alludes to, better times were to come, but first there was yet another battle at the bottom. Defeats to Bolton, Southampton and Spurs left Coventry looking over their shoulder as they entered April. Thankfully, a fine 1-0 win against Liverpool ended a run of three defeats on the spin just as it looked like City would be dragged kicking and screaming into the mire.

'That was a major game,' Daish admits. 'Noel scored. We were playing three at the back – me, Willo and Bussty. A cross came in and Noel stretched somehow at the near post to get it in. That was a great goal. Slowly but surely we were getting some momentum. I enjoyed playing against Liverpool. Everything was played in front of you and to feet. They never really tried to stretch you or get in behind you. That was such a big win for us, it was a massive boost. Coventry sometimes enjoyed being the underdog. There was always a good spirit in the camp at Coventry, even when results went against us. There was no blame culture within the squad.'

Team	P	GD	Pts
16. Southampton	34	-17	31
17. Manchester City	33	-24	31
18. Coventry	33	-20	30
19. QPR	33	-20	27

While we walked away from Highfield Road beaming, a dark day for the club was to come just days later. On Saturday, 8 April, Coventry travelled to Old Trafford. Even off the back of a win over Liverpool, an away fixture against Manchester United was a daunting task. City started on the front foot, winning a corner within the first two minutes. As the corner was swung in, defender Busst collided with United duo Denis Irwin and Brian McClair. The resulting injury has been well documented. Busst's leg was badly broken. The match was delayed by almost ten minutes as he was carefully placed on to a stretcher. Blood was mopped from the pitch. Peter Schmeichel was so traumatised he reportedly required counselling afterwards. The match was mere seconds old and Busst's career was, tragically, over. Today, Busst is refreshingly philosophical about the injury.

'I've never changed my opinion of it, it was just the worst timing,' he says. 'It was the way I just got caught between an inside and an outside tackle with all of us going for the ball. If any of the three of us had been out by 1/1,000th of a second, the injury wouldn't have happened. I'm an optimistic person and I had five great years at Coventry and I wouldn't change it for the world. If you're going to break your leg anywhere then do it at Old Trafford in front of however many thousands of people who were there. You hear a lot about players having a bubble lifestyle and struggling when they retire. I never had that bubble lifestyle. I worked from 16 years old in the real world, I already had that grounding and I knew football would end for me one day and I'd go back to reality.'

Midfielder Willie Boland had the unenviable task of coming off the bench to replace the stricken defender. With 88 minutes still to play, Boland admits that thoughts drifted as the afternoon went on.

'It was going through the motions until full time,' he admits. 'Don't get me wrong, everyone is still trying to win but the atmosphere was strange and you couldn't help but feel disappointment in the atmosphere. Dave is a top fella. He'd established himself in the team at that time, he'd been in the reserves and in and out of the team for a few years and he'd just got his chance. He deserved a longer career in the game.'

'It was a strange game,' Liam Daish concurs. 'The game was delayed for quite a while and for a while after no one really laid a glove on each other. I was right there with Bussty because he was alongside me at centre-half. We were playing alright. We had the corner and he went down. I went straight to him and he was in absolute distress. We lost 1-0 but the result didn't really matter.'

As Daish attests, a narrow defeat almost went unnoticed in the grand scheme of what had been witnessed that day. While such a focus on the career-ending injury that marred the match is perhaps understandable, Boland admits disappointment at the media coverage that followed.

'One of the most disappointing things for me was the following day in the centre-spread of the tabloids was a full colour picture of the injury,' he says. 'That was quite harrowing, especially if you're one of his team-mates or a family member. There was no need for that. It was awful.'

Busst faced a lengthy spell in hospital recuperating. To make matters worse, he contracted MRSA while in hospital and faced the very real possibility of losing his leg altogether as he endured operation after operation. Even in such desperate times, a little dark humour from the boss helped to raise his spirits.

'Ron came to see me in hospital,' he says. 'I was there in hospital with all of these pins and the first thing he said to me was, "You know what Bussty, you should have scored." That was Ron. Even in adversity he put a smile on my face.'

While Busst put up a brave fight to resume his career, it was not to be.

'It was about six months before I knew the full extent of the injury but I had an idea from the operations I was having,' he explains. 'I lost the tendons in my right leg and had something where my foot was kept at 90 degrees and I ended up with drop foot. It was that and the MRSA that stopped me playing again rather than the actual injury. I knew in myself after about three months that I wouldn't play again. When I was told, it was devastating news but it wasn't a big shock.'

It would have perhaps been understandable had the Sky Blues' season petered out from there. It's then a testament to the spirit in the squad that they went four unbeaten to secure survival for another year. A rare Eoin Jess goal proved the difference in a 1-0 win over QPR before a goalless draw against Nottingham Forest. A pair of Ndlovu goals in a 2-0 win over Wimbledon put safety into sight as they went into the final day of the season against Leeds. There was one relegation slot still to be decided and Coventry were in the mix with Manchester City and Southampton. The Sky Blues benefited from boasting a superior goal difference to Manchester City, so knew that if they bettered the result of their fellow Sky Blues then they would be safe. Despite that sliver of breathing room, it remained a nervy day for all in attendance at Highfield Road as Leeds came to town.

'It's a horrible situation,' Daish says of the final-day battle. 'Psychologically you don't play your normal game. You're on eggshells a little bit. It was nervy. Leeds didn't have anything to play for. Gary McAllister was playing for Leeds and he joined us the following season – I don't know if he knew he was on his way to us.'

One man lining up in midfield alongside McAllister that day was another future Sky Blue, Carlton Palmer. Palmer is adamant that it was business as usual, despite Leeds having little to play for.

'It's a football game, you just get on with it,' he says. 'You know a team in that situation is going to be up for it. At the end of the day, we had Howard Wilkinson and we were going out to win every football match. It didn't matter whether a team was going out to win the league, trying to stay in the league or if there was nothing to play for – it's three points. The mentality was the same. That mentality is always the same. Just go out there and win the game.'

It was just another match, but boy what a dull one it was. Ahead of the match I had optimistically predicted a 3-0 home win. Instead, a drab 0-0 draw was played out and Coventry survived on goal difference ahead of Southampton and the unfortunate souls who dropped out of the top flight that year, Manchester City. The most memorable part of the day came at Maine Road. With the scores tied at 2-2, City were given some duff information, which led them to believe that a draw was enough to keep them up. The resulting piece of time-wasting from midfielder Steve Lomas provided a big belly laugh for Big Ron.

'As soon as our game finished we ran straight down the tunnel and there were a few clubs still in the mix,' Ron says. 'Man City were drawing with Liverpool 2-2 and they got their wires mixed up and thought they were safe. Steve Lomas had the ball in the corner trying to waste time because they thought they were safe. We were laughing our heads off!'

There may have been laughter in the changing room, but there was also, once again, a feeling of disappointment. Coventry ended the season with just eight wins out of 38 league matches. There was a palpable feeling that things had to improve.

'We stayed up and the view was that we needed to be a lot better next year,' Daish says. 'We didn't want to be in that same position again.'

Team	P	GD	Pts
16. Coventry	38	-18	38
17. Southampton	38	-18	38
18. Manchester City (R)	38	-25	38

The sentiment of never again was evident once more. But, almost unbelievably, yet another final-day battle was on the horizon. This next fight, however, was perhaps the most dramatic in the club's history in a season that would see transformations on and off the pitch that would shape Coventry City for the rest of the decade.

6.

Gordon Takes Over

AFTER ANOTHER disappointing scrap at the end of the previous season, Coventry began the 1996/97 campaign with a feeling that something had to be done to ensure it didn't happen again. With Big Ron at the helm, Gordon Strachan in the wings and more money than ever before being pumped in, Coventry could no longer be a club that fought relegation year after year. While fans expected money to be spent on fresh blood, few expected the marquee name that arrived.

On 26 July 1996, Gary McAllister was unveiled as a Coventry City player. A league title winner just a few seasons earlier with Leeds, McAllister's £3m move was a gigantic statement of intent. According to Bryan Richardson, the club paid £1.5m up front, with the other half of the fee in staggered payments. McAllister signed a four-year contract.

Regardless of the finances, in terms of genuine star attraction, this was a mind-boggling transfer. Little old Coventry City, the perennial basement boys struggling at the foot of the table, had signed a creative powerhouse, a player in whom surely far 'bigger' clubs would have been interested. It wasn't just fans who were shocked at the signing. Some of the squad struggled to even get their heads around it.

'He walked in the door and you're like, "Bloody hell, that's Gary McAllister!"' says John Salako. 'It was a wow signing.

95

He was the leader on the pitch with Dion. That signing took us to another level, even in training.'

'I absolutely couldn't believe it,' attests Richard Shaw. 'When he rocked up, I was stunned. When someone like him joins your club it makes a big noise. You're thinking he's won a championship with Leeds and why was he coming to Coventry? Strach was a massive pull. McAllister coming, though, helped us probably keep Dion and helped us sign people like Roland Nilsson. When I watched Macca train and pass the ball, he was at another level. We used to do this thing in training where you'd work in twos and pass to each other, just pinging the ball and dropping it in. I'd always look for McAllister because I just wanted to learn from him. No one could manipulate a football like him. He could drop it in, he'd ping it, zing it, he had every pass in the book. It made our lives as centre-halves easier because when we got the ball we'd just give it to him because he was *the* player. Signing him was a massive coup. If anything, we weren't good enough for him at the time but just him being on the pitch pulled us up. He made us better and he probably doesn't even think that.'

While £3m for McAllister smashed the Sky Blues' transfer record, this was just a drop in the ocean with regards to what was going on elsewhere in the Premier League that summer. Middlesbrough, for example, splashed more than £8m on striker Fabrizio Ravanelli and handed him a staggering £42,000-per-week contract. Not for a second did I see Middlesbrough as a more attractive or established club than Coventry – they had only recently come back into the top flight, after all – but if this was the kind of money being thrown around then the McAllister deal looked small fry by comparison. The league was littered with big-money signings, whether it be Nottingham Forest spending £4.5m on Celtic's Pierre van Hooijdonk or Newcastle shelling out £15m for Alan Shearer. The Premier League riches had arrived and rival clubs were spending like there was no tomorrow. Despite this, McAllister certainly remained a landmark signing. But in a roundabout way he was actually responsible for the Sky Blues missing out on another midfield transfer target just before he signed on the dotted line.

'I'd been to watch Charlton,' Atkinson says, picking up the story. 'I'd had two of their players recommended to me. One was a centre-half called Richard Rufus and the other was Lee Bowyer. I thought they were both decent and the sort of players we should be taking. We couldn't afford the two of them so we went for Bowyer. He came to the training ground and we had a nice chat but Leeds came in for him. He said he appreciated what we were saying but he said he wanted to go to Leeds because he wanted to play with Gary McAllister. So he went to Leeds and I signed Gary McAllister! I have to say the McAllister deal was in many ways Gordon's influence. We looked after him very well, to be fair; I think we out-priced Liverpool on him. If Liverpool had signed him that year instead of us they'd have won the league.'

As several have already mentioned, the presence of McAllister's former Leeds team-mate Gordon Strachan proved a huge pull in attracting him to Highfield Road.

'A lot of that was to do with our friendship,' Strachan says of the transfer. 'Bryan Richardson liked to gamble on a player and he gambled on that. Gary was happy with the package that we put together. He had a wonderful spell. He's stubborn like me. We've been at loggerheads since the day we met, but we loved each other at the same time.'

Despite the high-profile signing, the Sky Blues once again started the season in dismal fashion. A friendly against Portuguese giants Benfica should have been a glamorous curtain-raiser but turned into a disaster as City were trounced 7-2. Things didn't get any better when the season kicked off with a 3-0 hammering at home to Nottingham Forest. Despite the Benfica debacle, confidence within the crowd was high going into the Forest fixture. This was a winnable match and we had our record signing ready to pull the strings in midfield.

'It was bang-bang-bang, we're three goals down and you're wondering where did that come from?' assesses no-nonsense centre-half Daish. 'It was a typical first game of the season. It could have easily been us 3-0 up. It was such an open game. Ron was calm after the game, he didn't get overly emotional after games. I saw him get a little bit mad but he wasn't a ranter and raver. He stayed quite calm. He'd been there, seen it and done it before. He was a calming presence. Gordon was probably more [emotional], as he was just starting out on that career.'

'We'd had a shocking pre-season,' Brian Borrows admits. 'Benfica had given us the absolute runaround. The writing was almost on the wall. We came up against Forest on the opening day, which looks like a winnable game, and you lose 3-0 and you're off to a terrible start.'

Fellow full-back David Burrows agrees with the assessment of Borrows, but alludes to deeper issues within that particular pre-season rather than just the 7-2 hammering.

'The pre-season was far too difficult,' he says. 'We started the season with problems. My season was dogged by injury and that was through me not having the right physical condition. I was an explosive player, not someone who could run around all day. We'd overdone it. By the time we'd recovered from the pre-season, two-thirds of the season was gone and we were in a mess. Nottingham Forest used to have a light pre-season and always seemed to be fresh and start the season well, but then it took its toll on them after Christmas. By this point I'd got quite a lot of experience with pre-seasons but this pre-season was ruthless. I didn't enjoy it. That's my personal view, some players might have enjoyed it. You need time to recover and I don't think we did.'

Whether an over-exuberant pre-season was at fault or not, the facts were that the Sky Blues made a stinking start to the campaign. For all his class, and despite heading his first goal for the club in just his second match, against West Ham, McAllister struggled to gel with his new team-mates in the early part of the season. Atkinson has a theory now for what may have gone wrong.

'I made a mistake with Gary,' Atkinson concedes. 'He's a great pro and a great player but I made a mistake by making him captain straightaway. I know a lot of the lads were looking at him and at first he didn't really settle into the Coventry thing. That was not his fault. I shouldn't have made him captain straightaway. He was the captain but I shouldn't have made him captain straightaway. I think it affected Dion a bit. I should have left it a bit. It's like when I went to Man United, I didn't make Bryan Robson captain straightaway, I left it for a while and then eased him into it. I should have done the same with McAllister.'

I must at this point note that of all the players I've spoken to for this book, none have suggested any issue with McAllister and his taking of the captaincy. Nonetheless, something wasn't quite clicking. The adage of a single player not making a team comes into Richard Shaw's assessment of what was going wrong.

'Signing McAllister was good but he doesn't make a team,' he says. 'Look at the sides in the league that season. Those Manchester United and Arsenal sides were sensational but then someone like Middlesbrough went and signed Ravanelli and Juninho. It's a tough league to compete in. It's easy to say we should have been mid-table but you're talking about teams that were just way, way better than us. For us to compete technically, tactically and physically was difficult. We had a poor start. We lost 4-0 against Middlesbrough and it kicked off in the changing room afterwards. Gary Mac was vocal in the changing room afterwards about us needing to be better. That was a turning point for us. When you don't start well in the first six games, you're playing catch-up all of the time. We had that start and we were short of self-belief.'

Poor decisions did little to help that crisis of self-belief as tempers boiled over in a controversial 2-0 defeat to Chelsea. With just under half an hour played, a Steve Ogrizovic throw down the pitch was clearly handled by Chelsea's Dan Petrescu. It was a blatant handball witnessed by everyone inside Stamford Bridge – except referee Paul Danson and his assistants. From the resulting move, Frank Leboeuf put the home team ahead. Several minutes of furious arguing between most of the Coventry team and bench and Danson ensued. The result was Liam Daish being given a red card for overstepping the mark with his critique of the referee's performance. Atkinson, Strachan and coach Garry Pendrey were all apoplectic, seething and seemingly close to spitting blood at the officials. Watching on during those years, I often wondered who the good cop in the managerial team was, particularly within the Strachan–Pendrey relationship. Both seemed intimidating figures on the touchline, either one at any second ready to bark in the ear of officials, the opposition and, quite often, their own players. It seems, however, that for Pendrey at least, his bark was far worse than his bite.

'He was a funny man and a good coach,' Salako says of the former Birmingham defender. 'He worked a lot with the shape, the back four and midfield. He was very light-hearted and good with Strach because you need that good cop, bad cop. In the dugout he would get involved and be aggressive because you needed to be. He was a winner. When he crossed that white line, he would be the first one there when he had to be. I'm not sure if he could fight if he had to. He acted like he could fight, that's the thing to do, you've got to act like you can fight [laughs].'

Ahead of an away trip to Everton for a night match live on Sky, City had won just one of their first 11 in the league. The club had amassed a measly eight points from those matches and sat 19th in the table, four points ahead of a Blackburn team yet to register a win. Rumours were rife that Atkinson was about to step aside and allow Strachan to take charge earlier than planned. A 1-1 draw with the Toffees wasn't enough to quell the goings-on behind the scenes and soon Atkinson was gone. Well, not quite gone; the original story was that he had agreed to move into a director-of-football-style role while Strachan took over as manager. However, it seems that not all in the boardroom were on the same page with the story.

'We had a bad run,' says Bryan Richardson. 'Ron wasn't well because his father, who was a lovely man, was really quite poorly. I said to Ron that we would put the onus on him and say that he thought now was the right time for Gordon to take over and then there would be no loss of face. I said we would say he would become director of football and it could all be handled smoothly.'

Unfortunately, things didn't go as smoothly as planned. Word of the decision was leaked, with some of the tabloids seemingly finding out before Ron. Atkinson has his own views on the moment that he thinks he became a dead man walking.

'I think I was the last person to know,' he sighs. 'Somebody told me off-hand. I said, "You what?!" I'll tell you what I think happened. Something happened when Geoffrey Robinson came on the board. It was Arsène Wenger's first home game at Arsenal and after the game there was an old journalist Ken Jones and he pulled me in the marble halls at Highbury. We were talking away and Geoffrey Robinson was shouting me and I was in the middle of talking to the press guys and I said, "Geoffrey, just leave it." I knew as soon as I said it that I'd upset him. The week after I was moved upstairs. There was no directive at all. I didn't have any directives from the club so I went my own way for a while. I would come in occasionally and the players would have a bit of a laugh when I came in. I really don't know what happened. I thought we were playing better and I had a sense that we were starting to become decent.'

While results had been poor, Atkinson had remained a largely popular figure within the club. It's little surprise then, and no slight against his replacement, that some players were sad to see the former Villa man go.

'Ron's father was ill and that was difficult for him,' David Burrows recalls. 'He took a little bit of time out to deal with that, so Gordon came and took more responsibility for the team. From my point of view, I thought Ron and Gordon had different ideas on what they wanted to do. Gordon was more tactical, disciplined and wanted to coach a lot more. Ron wanted to play, he didn't want to see too much of the tactical side and wanted players to just enjoy the game. I missed Ron. I missed his dressing-room presence and his jokes. Don't get me wrong though, if you stepped out of line with Ron he'd come down on you like a ton of bricks. You didn't mess with Ron.'

'We drew against Everton and after that Ron told us he was going,' remembers Liam Daish. 'We never really got to the bottom of it. All I knew was the next day Ron came back to take us all out for lunch for his leaving do. That probably doesn't happen now but Ron was renowned for his leaving do and taking the lads out. I think the day ended up becoming quite eventful. That's another story. The club was ready for Gordon to take things on to the next level, which he did. Gordon had the respect of the players from day one. He already had our respect as a player and an assistant. Gordon's game was being out on the grass. Ron was more of one who would take you to one side, have a word with you and make you feel great. Gordon was the technician.'

Stuart Linnell believes that, despite the dips in form, Atkinson deserved a level of respect for what he brought to the club. Here, after all, was a man who delivered 5,000 more fans through the Highfield Road gates at a stroke. A manager who oversaw signings that, only a few years previously, Coventry fans could have only dreamt of.

'I think Ron feels he left the club sooner than he would have liked,' says Linnell. 'Because he was Ron, he'd been able to attract players to the club that we wouldn't otherwise have been able to. The likes of Strachan and Gary McAllister. They came into Coventry, at least partly, because of Ron. It's been in the history of Coventry that, whatever the make-up of the board, there's never been significant financial backing for any manager in the history of the club. That's why Bobby had his little black book. We've never had that team of absolute winners because the resources were never quite there. If Ron had the financial backing in Coventry that had been available to him at other clubs then I think it would have been a very different story.'

For others, Ron's sacking was inevitable, particularly at a club not blessed with a squad full of genuinely world-class players. In such a case, dips in form will always be a factor. Such teams are characterised by their lack of consistency and Coventry were, and always have been, no different.

'It went through the usual scenario with Coventry where you go through a good phase but it's difficult to sustain it,' suggests Willie Boland. 'Then, when you're not going through that good phase it's about reacting to that. Once again, similarly to Phil, that happened again with Ron. Results weren't going great and a change had to be made.'

The change was made. Out went Atkinson, in came Strachan, stepping up from assistant to manager. It came as little surprise to those already at the club that Strachan put an emphasis on the fitness side of the game. Here was a seasoned veteran whose game had been built on backing up his undoubted quality on the ball with limitless effort off it.

'He was in his late thirties but he was the fittest person in the squad,' recalls Brian Borrows. 'The physical stuff that we did was very intense. That was Gordon. He put a big emphasis on the physical conditioning of the players. That was his biggest thing that you would notice. There was an intensity to how you trained. It was quite obsessive at times. Gordon wanted us to be the fittest team in the league, quite rightly. Some of the physical sessions we did with Gordon were very different to what we had done in the past. We had some very fit players like Paul Telfer and Noel Whelan, naturally fit lads. No disrespect, you wouldn't play under Gordon if you didn't have a certain level of fitness. You wouldn't have seen Micky Quinn playing under Gordon! Gordon was in his early days as a manager when I was there. I'd have liked to have worked with him when I was younger, to be able to see what he could do to take me to a different level as a player, fitness-wise. I had gone past my best by the time Gordon got there because age does catch up with you.'

'Training and preparation for games changed massively,' Daish adds. 'Gordon as a coach would try and set out preparation for who we were playing but then Ron was one of those where he liked to come out and get a five-a-side pitch sorted, get involved and have the banter. You sensed that Gordon wanted to take more control regarding the preparation of who we were playing against. You could definitely see the change.'

It wasn't just fitness that was the focus for Strachan. His eagerness to improve even the most senior of pros was evident from the off.

'I saw Gordon's enthusiasm and that he wanted to improve players,' Steve Ogrizovic recalls. 'He played his career like that, he was an outstanding footballer. I preferred playing with him than against him! He had this uncanny way of being able to control the referee as a player, he had a great wit and you could see that when he came on to the coaching staff. He had the year with Ron Atkinson, who showed him the way into management, and when he did step up he was different to the managers that we had before, he would don the tracksuit and was very big into the coaching and trying to improve players. That's exactly what he did.'

All of a sudden, this new-look squad who had been signed by Atkinson, the likes of Burrows, Richardson, Shaw, Daish and Salako, were faced with a change of leader and a very different approach under Strachan.

'Most of us had signed for Ron and he was such a great character,' Salako says. 'Strachan was doing the coaching. Strach is a soldier. He is a driving force. He's all about work rate, whereas Ron was more about man-management. Strach was finding his way and he would drive us hard. I remember we would do training in the morning and then do set pieces in the afternoon. I would take set pieces from both sides. I might hit a couple of dodgy ones and Strach would say, "One more dodgy one and we're all going for a run." The lads would look at me. I'd try to whip one across the six-yard box and I'd duff one in and Strach would say, "Right, if you're not going to do it properly, we're all going for a run." We'd all go for a run and the lads would be like, "Bloody hell, Sal." Strach was demanding, he had very high levels. Ron was more jovial and joking. Strachan was very serious but it was still enjoyable. He got the best out of us and we enjoyed the hard work and the drive. Strach could be difficult at times and there would be stand-up rows after games. He would come in and take the paint off the walls. He was a fiery, demanding character but he was fair.'

Strachan was able to successfully demand so much from his players from day one due to having their complete respect. As a player, he had been there, seen it and done it. Even as he approached 40, he was still the best player at the club. A little while down the line he would be joined at Coventry by his son Gavin, who turned out first for the youth team and then later clocked up 16 first-team appearances. Strachan Jr was acutely aware of his dad's talent and the respect that he commanded from his new squad.

'He would join in with the youth team sessions and at 40 years old he was far better than all of us!' Gavin says with a laugh. 'He would ping a 60-yard pass first time.'

Gordon certainly had the playing ability, but you need plenty more to your repertoire if you're going to make it as a Premier League manager.

'His playing career gave him the initial respect but that only lasts so long,' Gavin continues. 'He was respected because of how detailed his training sessions were and he treated the players like men, not like children. There was a mutual respect and honesty. He had what would now be called a leadership group: Paul Williams, Richard Shaw, Gary McAllister, Dion Dublin. They maintained the culture and the environment that was required from my old man.'

Even players who had signed for Atkinson and had professed their love of playing for the larger-than-life gaffer immediately saw the benefits that Strachan could bring.

'I really enjoyed working with Ron,' says Richard Shaw. 'I enjoyed the training and everything about him. You can only speak as you find, and I enjoyed working under Ron. He was a very good man-manager. He was used to big characters and big teams. Maybe we needed a wee bit more tactically and that's when Strachs took over and did a bit more of that. Strachs was great; when people speak about the kind of training Wenger and Mourinho introduced – Strachs was doing that in 1997. Under Strachan, I went from being known as a man-to-man marker and getting tight to people to becoming quite comfortable on the ball and happy to play out. Gordon massively improved my game, all around. Working on things like dropping balls into Dion. What Strachs did was he improved players. Every single person that he coached, he improved. I won player of the year in 1999 and that was down to Strachan. Alongside Steve Coppell, Strachan was the best manager I worked with.'

'Gordon was a super coach,' agrees David Burrows. 'At my age then, I was still learning things from Gordon. He added little bits and bobs to my game. It's a pity I didn't get Gordon when I was 18 because I regard him as the best coach I ever worked with. We were much more disciplined and tactical; maybe some of Ron's flair went out of the window.'

He may have had the respect of the players, but that didn't instantly translate on to the pitch. The Gordon Strachan era began in distinctly underwhelming fashion. A 2-2 draw with high-flying Wimbledon – featuring a stupendous goal from Whelan as he volleyed in a sublime McAllister pass – was followed by three defeats: to Aston Villa, Derby and Spurs. Coventry needed a lift. They found one from a signing that proved to be one of Atkinson's final acts for the club. Atkinson and Strachan capitalised on Kevin Keegan's well-documented and utterly bizarre decision to scrap Newcastle United's reserves. With fringe players no longer able to play their way into the manager's thoughts, many were looking for pastures new. One such player was Darren Huckerby, who found himself behind the likes of Shearer, Beardsley and Ferdinand in the pecking order at St James' Park. Bryan Richardson recalls that, while Big Ron was still in charge when the agreement was rubber-stamped, Strachan was once again a big part in the deal. Richardson and Strachan went to watch Huckerby play while he was on loan with Millwall. They came away impressed enough to put the wheels in motion for a £750,000 move.

However, before the deal was sealed, Huckerby was invited to take part in a trial match that saw the Sky Blues travel to Jersey to face a Jersey Select XI. The striker certainly impressed as he bagged a hat-trick in the match, but today jokes that wasn't a particularly impressive achievement as 'Richard Shaw scored in that game, so that shows you how good the opposition must have been!' That man Shaw was impressed by what he saw from the new boy.

'Shortly after I joined, Darren Huckerby joined and he was a maverick,' says Shaw. 'He got the ball and just did what he wanted to do – and it worked! He had absolute pace. When you have Whelan, Dublin and Huckerby combining up front, you're always going to score goals.'

Goals were exactly what Huckerby brought to the party, but points remained hard to come by. He came off the bench and made a goal for Dublin in a 2-1 defeat to the Villa on his debut. Defeats against Derby and Spurs followed and things were looking bleak.

Team	P	GD	Pts
18. Southampton	17	-8	13
19. Coventry	16	-13	10
20. Nottingham Forest	15	-13	9

Then came Huckerby's breakthrough as he bagged his first goal in his third start for the club, a night match against, you guessed it, his former employers Newcastle United. The Highfield Road faithful were left awestruck by the direct Huckerby's blistering pace. A Kevin Richardson pass in the middle of the park left Huckerby still with plenty to do, but he shot past Philippe Albert and squeezed the ball past the oncoming Pavel Srnicek to score his first Coventry City goal with the match just six minutes old. With 30 minutes on the clock, Richardson again released Huckerby, who this time laid the ball into the path of Gary McAllister. The skipper swept the ball home to double his team's lead. Coventry ended up 2-1 winners. A new star had arrived at Highfield Road.

'From a defender's point of view, [Huckerby] was one that was a constant threat,' Liam Daish adds. 'He had pace but he was a strong boy as well. He had good upper-body strength and could hold players off. If he got the other side of a defender then they weren't getting back at him. As a defender playing alongside Darren it was great because you could hit hopeful balls or clearances and he would get you up the pitch with his willingness to chase after lost causes. He retained the ball well and gave us a threat. He was a Jamie Vardy sort of player, just looking to get on the other side of defenders.'

'We had a bond, me and Huckerby,' says Richard Shaw, continuing the Huckerby love-in. 'I absolutely loved him. We used to buzz off his banter. He used to come in with Kevin Richardson and Kevin used to hammer him. He was absolutely rapid. If you've got pace in the Premier League, even now, you will stand out. I used to watch him and think, "Darren, what are you doing?" He'd turn past three defenders, run into one, get a ricochet and then score! He was a genius. He was technically, not sure. Tactically, not sure. But put the ball at his feet and he would do what he wants. His pace was a joke but his upper-body strength was also incredible, people would bounce off him. What a brilliant signing.'

The Dublin–Huckerby partnership looked the business from the off, even if Dublin found himself moved into defence at times during the season.

'You take over as a manager and think you know what the problem is and you can sort it right away – wrong,' Strachan says. 'We lost three of my first four games. The first one we won was Newcastle when they were up at the top of the league. That was when Huckerby came in. Huckerby and Dion were great together. Around that time we changed to three centre-halves and Dion went back to centre-half. We stopped goals to give us a chance of winning. This was [assistant manager] Alex Miller's idea. I went with it. We came good and won four on the trot.'

Many centre-forwards would have their nose put squarely out of joint by being asked to play at centre-half, but Dublin is adamant that he was happy to do whatever was required for the cause.

'Playing at centre-half didn't bother me at all,' he says. 'It hindered me with goalscoring, of course, but the mindset of a player from my era is all about how can you best contribute and help the team? Scoring the goals was great when I was up top but when I was in defence it was all about stopping them and putting your body on the line. I didn't mind doing that at all. If I was needed at centre-half I would just do it, I wouldn't ask any questions. That was Gordon Strachan's influence; he was possibly the best coach I had in my 22 years as a player. He was outstanding. He looked after the team, he cared and he trusted us. If he was to put a team together right now, he would pick eight or nine of that Coventry side – 100 per cent. He trusts us and we trust him.'

Wins over Leicester, Leeds and Middlesbrough followed, and all of a sudden Strachan seemed to be finding this management lark an absolute doddle. It was almost nosebleed territory as the club jumped up to 12th in the table. Stuart Linnell recalls the squad buying into the new man's methods right from the off.

'The joke would go around when we interviewed Strachan that people would ask us to put up subtitles so they could understand his Scottish accent,' he says. 'There was no doubt that the players understood what he was saying and wanted them to do, though. I remember one pre-season it was a horrible day of weather and pouring with rain. All of the players came in soaked through and miserable and the last one in was Gordon. He was absolutely caked in mud, socks around his ankles, hair completely soaked. He came in, clapped his hands, rubbed them together and said, "This is what it's like, this is the real game, this is what we have to understand." He was telling the team to roll their sleeves up, work together and be part of the team. That's what he wanted and to a very large degree he was successful in that.'

That Middlesbrough match was notable for more than just the three points that the Sky Blues acquired. It also saw Steve Ogrizovic break the club's all-time appearance record, overtaking George Curtis as he turned out for Coventry for the 544th time.

'I was very lucky that I had a body that withstood all of the training and the things the body has to go through to be a professional athlete,' Oggy says, searching for an explanation for his longevity. 'I had quite a robust body, I was very rarely injured. I started professional football in 1977 and I don't think I missed a game through injury until 1989. I was lucky with injuries but also back then you played with more knocks than you would do now. There wasn't the policy of rotating goalkeepers back then either.'

Many interviewees for this book have spoken of Oggy's dedication. It was no accident that he ended up playing well into his forties. He was able to do so because he put in the hard miles.

'For training sessions Oggy would be out there at 10am before everyone else,' says club legend Trevor Peake, who returned as a coach in the late '90s. 'He'd take a couple of youth players out. That was when he was 35 or 36. His preparation for games was incredible. He was a top goalkeeper. He was dedicated to the game. He was just a top professional. You want to show him to young players and show them how he got where he got and how many games he played. He got everything he could from his ability and his attitude was unquestionable.'

'I enjoyed training more than playing games probably,' Oggy adds. 'I used to love going in every day. From an early age I felt the more I practised the better I would become. Sometimes now I look back and think I overtrained at times. I felt I had to train because mentally I was in the best place possible if I put the work in on the training ground. That worked for me. When you look at Coventry and the number of years at the top level, to have achieved that feat and overtake a legend like George Curtis ... I know the esteem he was held in at this club. To play more games for the football club at the highest level meant so much and it still means so much to me now.'

With his seasoned goalkeeper still doing the business at one end and his new-found goalscorer ripping defences to shreds, Strachan could have been forgiven for thinking that his influence on the pitch was no longer required and his playing days would now be over. This wasn't quite the case. He was jolted back down to earth rather quickly. After four victories on the spin, along came a run of three without a win, including a 4-0 thumping against relegation-threatened Blackburn. Even worse, that run saw Dublin pick up back-to-back red cards – one against Sunderland, followed immediately by one in the Blackburn thrashing. This meant that the Sky Blues' talisman would miss seven matches (as it turned out this would be three FA Cup ties and four league fixtures). It was time for drastic measures and Strachan was back on the bench for a 1-0 win over Nottingham Forest and came on as a sub for the final nine minutes in a 2-1 defeat against Aston Villa. This would be one of several occasions that the gaffer found himself back on the team sheet towards the back end of the 1996/97 season.

'I kept myself fit and played reserve games, and in those games I could move people into position, cajole them and demand from them,' Strachan says. 'When Ron left I thought, "Great, I don't have to play again!" When I was manager I had people like Gary McAllister and Kevin Richardson in my ear telling me I should play again. That was hard work. Being a Premier League manager and playing. I was falling asleep in my office. In the afternoons I was collapsed at my desk. I remember coming on for Coventry when we were 2-0 down at Southampton and I went in midfield with Kevin and Gary – it was the oldest midfield of all time!'

Even the veterans in midfield were struggling to steady the ship and the Sky Blues were on a collision course with a relegation battle. Yet another relegation battle. As it turned out, it would be the most nerve-wracking scrap in the club's history.

7.

The Great Escape

COVENTRY HAVE a reputation for being expert escapologists when it comes to Premier League survival, hence Big Ron once saying, 'If the *Titanic* had been painted sky blue it would have stayed up.' If we're talking by-the-seat-of-your-pants escapes though, the end to the 1996/97 season takes some beating.

Gordon Strachan's honeymoon period was well and truly over and a run of eight games without a win left City staring down the barrel. Even worse, goals were being shipped left, right and centre. A 4-0 hammering at the hands of Newcastle was followed by a superb John Hartson performance as West Ham swept the Sky Blues aside with relative ease at Highfield Road. As we entered April, City had slipped into the drop zone and, with Liverpool, Chelsea, Arsenal and Spurs still to play, it was becoming miracle time. Some intervention came from an unlikely source – BBC commentator John Motson, who, after working on the defeat to West Ham for *Match of the Day*, gave his old mate Big Ron a call.

'[Motson] rang me and said if I didn't do something they were going to get relegated,' Ron says. 'The next game was Liverpool away. I spoke to Gordon and said, "Little man, you're in trouble, if you carry on like this you're going to go down." He said he thought I was probably right. I had an unbelievable record at Anfield. With Man United I went there seven or eight times and lost once. I won there with Villa and Coventry. I said, "You know what I'm like at Anfield, I'll come give you a hand if you want.'"

David Burrows, who had won a league title with Liverpool in 1990, was given a slightly unfamiliar role that day, moving across from left-back to centre-half, playing in a back three alongside Richard Shaw and Paul Williams.

'I marked Stan Collymore,' he recalls. 'I spoke to Ron before the match. He was in the stands that day and he said, "You keep him quiet and we can win this." We had goals in the team. You always have to believe. When you lose that belief, you're done.'

One man who may have lost a little belief ahead of the match was Liverpool manager Roy Evans. That certainly seemed to be the case once he laid eyes upon City's special guest for the day.

'We get there and Roy Evans sees me and says, "Oh fucking hell, the albatross is here,"' Ron says. 'I was giving it the whole "this place has never been a problem".'

As it turned out, on that occasion Anfield wasn't a problem. Admittedly, it didn't seem that way when Robbie Fowler rifled a shot past Steve Ogrizovic on 52 minutes to give the hosts the lead. Perhaps the albatross had lost his touch. But City remained resolute in the face of almost total domination from Liverpool and eventually reaped the rewards when a Noel Whelan header from a McAllister corner looked to have earned a draw. With seven minutes to play, Strachan came on to help guard what may have been a valuable point.

'I was a substitute that day,' says Strachan. 'I started in the directors' box and then I jumped from the box into the stand. I went for a warm-up but really I was working with the defence to keep them pushed up. [Liverpool coach] Ronnie Moran was complaining to the referee and giving me stick and I was giving him plenty back. As we got on the bus after the game he was still shouting at me, calling me a cheeky this and that. Eventually in that game I went on to shore things up and get a draw that might help us.'

But then with 90 minutes played, McAllister stood over another corner – and he had a decision to make. Strachan recalls that he and the skipper discussed whether to keep the ball in the corner and safeguard the point or chuck it into the mixer and go for broke. Fortunately, they opted for the latter. McAllister's lofted corner bamboozled future England No.1 David James, who flapped hopelessly at the ball, leaving Dion Dublin to tap home from just about on the goal line. A tactical masterclass, then? Not quite, says Strachan.

'It's hilarious – after a game like that a commentator will say you got your tactics spot on,' he says. 'You'll look at them and say, "Really? They had 36 shots at goal! Do you think I practised letting them having 36 shots at goal and us having two?!" It's a ludicrous statement, like we would plan to stay in our own half for almost the whole game!'

Regardless of the tactics, the result was huge for both clubs. It provided a massive boost for City's survival hopes. But it also put a dent in Liverpool's title charge as a win would have sent them to the top of the table. The ramifications of the 90 minutes were not lost on Big Ron.

'We were at the bottom of the league and they were near the top. If we'd have lost we'd have dropped out and they'd have won the league,' he predicts. 'That result swung the whole thing around.'

Steve Ogrizovic, a man who had seen it and done it so many times before, agrees with Atkinson's appraisal of how important the Liverpool victory was.

'We were a resilient team and we had times throughout the years where we were at the bottom and we had to find a way to stay up,' Ogrizovic says. 'Even though it might be different players, you had that character within the club and within the fans as well. The fans were great in times of trouble, knowing we could do it, and the players buy into that.

We had to go to Liverpool and we were in real trouble. I don't know how we managed to score two goals late on and turn it around into a win. The belief we got from that result helped carry us through the rest of the games.'

After the win at Anfield, a miracle was perhaps no longer needed to ensure survival, but a slice of luck was still required. Ahead of their visit to Highfield Road, just three days after that energy-sapping Liverpool win, Chelsea's kit man delivered said piece of luck. The Ruud Gullit-led west Londoners arrived for the night match with only their home kit. With their royal blue kit and City's sky blue and dark blue stripes, it seemed that there was only one outcome – Gordon Strachan's men would have to wear their away kit. Strachan didn't agree.

'They turned up, typical Chelsea, the arrogance was seeping off them as they came off the bus with their sunglasses on. It was night time for Christ's sake!' Strachan remembers with a laugh. 'Everything about them reeked of arrogance. The referee asked if we had a second strip. I said, "We certainly have got a second strip, but we're not going to wear it." There was a meeting with me and Ruud and he was throwing his arms about saying we needed to change. I said, "No, let's look at the rules." It said we didn't have to change, they had to change. It all kicked off in the dressing room. The referee was asking what to do. I said, "I'll tell you what we have got, we've got this strip, it's an awful red and purple thing." We gave them that and we could hear them raging in the dressing room, screaming and shouting. They were saying, "Why should we change? They've got three other strips!" Well yes, we did have three strips, but we weren't changing for them. So, I was shouting back at them through the dressing room door.'

The verbal sparring didn't end once the match kicked off either, as Strachan recalls.

'I played in that game and they were all moaning and groaning at me,' he says. 'I was playing while having to verbally joust with the Chelsea guys. I was going up to them, saying, "You look absolutely fantastic in this." They were wearing our top with their own shorts. It was probably the worst strip anybody could possibly create.'

There was an air of confusion among the Highfield Road faithful as the visitors trotted out in the home team's shirts. At first, I glanced at my dad, wondering whether we had made some new signings that we hadn't heard about. It quickly became evident that this wasn't the case; we may have splashed a bit more cash in recent years but Zola, Gullit and co. were still way out of our price bracket! Some players had attempted to cover up the Coventry badge on the shirt, others hadn't bothered. Unsurprisingly, most seemed embarrassed at their Frankenstein's monster of an outfit for the evening. Perhaps the only thing more awful than Chelsea's hotchpotch kit that night was their performance. One thing that falls against that narrative, however, is that the visitors actually took the lead. Two minutes before half-time, Paul Hughes bundled in a goal ugly enough to befit the strip he was wearing after some less than commanding defending in the box. At the interval it was looking like an off-colour Chelsea could take the points and undo all the good work done at Anfield 72 hours earlier. However, inspired by their Energizer Bunny-like player-manager, Coventry came out all guns blazing in the second half and brushed Chelsea aside with three goals in nine minutes. Dublin levelled the scores after a Teddy-Sheringham-to-Alan-Shearer-esque lay-off from Noel Whelan, before a Paul Williams header gave City the lead. The win was wrapped up when a long ball from Strachan led to some comical defending from Frank Leboeuf and stand-in Chelsea goalkeeper Frode Grodas, allowing Whelan to poke the ball into an unguarded net from 25 yards.

The kit mix-up meant Chelsea played the match without names on the back of their shirts, and as an observer in the East Stand that night it was difficult to believe that this really was soon-to-be World Cup winner Leboeuf and co. That man Leboeuf's main act of the night was to throw his makeshift shirt on to the Highfield Road pitch in disgust come the final whistle. Full-back David Burrows thinks the pre-match fashion faux pas put Chelsea's megastars off their game.

'That was incredible,' he laughs. 'They didn't want to wear our kit! Little things like this, it's amazing how it happened at that time when we needed the points. Chelsea were upset but that was their problem. They never played that night, we were worthy winners. Little things like that turn people's mentalities. This was a team of stars, they were Chelsea, they didn't want to wear our shirts. I think that gave us an edge and gave them an excuse, it unsettled them. For a player to throw a shirt on the floor, that's pathetic and it summed up their evening.'

'It's funny what can get into players' heads,' adds Brian Borrows. 'It can be any old excuse like, "This kit is crap, I don't like the colour of it, it's too baggy, it's not the same quality or whatever." All of a sudden that is affecting their performance, which it really shouldn't with top players. We took every advantage. You can thrive on things like that.'

Richard Shaw, who lined up as one of three defenders against Liverpool and then in a back four for the Chelsea match, attributes a big part of those six points to his gaffer.

'We had Liverpool and Chelsea within three days and Strachan played a part in both games, even though he was about 42 or something! We were begging him to play because he was such a good player. His pace was gone but he had this thought process of how to slow a game down and how to up the tempo when we needed it – there was no one better. To win those two games was monumental, absolutely huge for us staying up. That Chelsea game, Highfield Road under the lights was just fantastic.'

Coventry had come into the match still looking for their first home win of the calendar year. We may have been almost halfway through April, but it was well worth the wait. However, the real drama was still to come.

Back-to-back draws with first Southampton and then Arsenal propelled City to the relatively dizzy heights of 16th as we approached the penultimate match of the season, a home fixture with Derby County. The Rams had more of an eye on a late surge into the top half of the table rather than worrying about what was going on below them but, nevertheless, no doubt buoyed by the impressive recent form of four matches unbeaten, the Sky Blues went into the fixture with many fans thinking it would be the day that Premier League survival was guaranteed for another year. I, for one, was certainly confident that we would follow up those fantastic wins against Liverpool and Chelsea with another three points here. Such hopes faded when defender Gary Rowett's free kick was diverted by the head of Burrows past Ogrizovic. Nine minutes later, referee Roger Dilkes handed the Sky Blues a lifeline when he adjudged Christian Dailly to have fouled Dublin in the box and, in fairness, Dailly was climbing all over the City striker. McAllister stepped up for the pressure penalty and dispatched it confidently, sending Mart Poom the wrong way. It was at this point, as we watched on at Highfield Road, that my dad turned to me and said, 'One point isn't enough, we have to win.' In a rare state of pessimism from my 11-year-old self, I replied, 'It's more important that we just don't lose.' With 67 minutes on the clock, my doom and gloom outlook was proven, for once, to be well-founded. Poom unleashed an almighty punt down the middle of the park that parted the centre of defence like Moses at the Red Sea. Dean Sturridge nipped in and lofted the ball over Ogrizovic and into the net. The air and life was instantly sucked out of Highfield Road. This was our chance, our opportunity to guarantee survival and we had let it slip away from our grasp. We sat in our seats motionless, in silence, unable to process what had just happened. It wasn't just the fans, the players also knew that they had just snatched defeat from the jaws of victory.

'We put ourselves in a difficult position by losing to Derby; we could have been safe,' recalls Richard Shaw. 'On the drive home I was in the car with my then wife and I didn't say a word to her for about an hour and a half on the way home. We were supposed to be going out with friends that night and I said, "I'm not going out." I thought we were relegated. We should never have lost to Derby, that was our opportunity to really get ourselves safe.'

Shaw's defensive comrade David Burrows agrees, adding, 'That knocked us back. In the dressing room afterwards it was a real setback for us. We had to win. We knew we had to go to Tottenham so that Derby game had to be a win, so when it didn't go that way we were deflated, no doubt about it. We had to pick ourselves up and go again.'

While the defeat was bad enough in isolation, what really delivered the hammer blow was the fact that all three of City's relegation rivals – West Ham, Middlesbrough and Sunderland – picked up three points apiece. Suddenly, Coventry slipped from 16th and with safety in sight, to 19th and needing to better the final-day result of both Sunderland and Middlesbrough to stay up. In fact, they would have gone into the final match already down had Bryan Robson's 'Boro not had three points docked for failing to fulfil a fixture with Blackburn due to injuries.

Team	P	GD	Pts
17. Sunderland	37	-17	40
18. Middlesbrough	37	-9	38
19. Coventry	37	-17	38

Picking the players up again after such a gut-wrenching set of results fell on the shoulders of Strachan. Not an easy task for a manager who had been through the rigours of end-of-season stresses time and time again, so for a boss in his first season in charge it was perhaps an unrealistic ask to expect him to somehow lift his troops. He did so, however, through the old footballing cliché of taking things one match at a time.

'It was difficult to raise everyone, including myself, after that game,' he admits. 'I said to myself on the Sunday that I was going to go in and, if anybody was worrying, I told them, "Look, let's not worry about relegation. If it happens, worry then. The next five days let's just have a bit of fun, concentrate, work hard and see where we go. Everything else is out of our hands." What was the use in worrying? When something happens then you deal with it. There was no use in using nervous energy at that point. Before that game, it was the usual, I told the players to free themselves to play and not to come off with regrets. We played with freedom until the last 15 minutes. The last thing I said was not to worry about relegation because it hadn't happened yet.'

With that, the club prepared for possibly its biggest match since the 1987 FA Cup Final. They would face Spurs at White Hart Lane on 11 May 1997, the final day of the 1996/97 season. They knew that even a win might not be enough, depending on results elsewhere. Stuart Linnell saw comparisons between those two seismic battles with Spurs that came a decade apart.

'So many times in the history of Coventry City you think the game's up,' he says. 'Even in the cup final in 1987. We'd got to the final and there we were conceding a goal in the opening minutes. It was easy to think, "Oh well, at least we're having a day out at Wembley." Then for it to unfold as it did was sensational, and the same thing applied in many ways to the game at White Hart Lane. It was a huge challenge. We were all trying to convince ourselves that it would be okay, but nobody really believed it.'

One man who believed that he could make the difference on the day was Noel Whelan.

'I was excited for that game because I wanted to be the star man on the day,' he says. 'It was a big game and I wanted to play in big games. When you look at the players we had there's no way we should have been in a relegation battle, but we were.'

Despite their fate ultimately being out of their hands, Richard Shaw attests to the surprisingly calm atmosphere around Ryton in the build-up to the final-day showdown.

'I always thought we would beat Tottenham but we still had to rely on two other results,' he admits. 'Strach was great that week. There was no drama, we didn't have ten meetings telling us what Tottenham do, because we watched them all the time anyway, we knew what they were all about. The key thing was keeping our feet on the ground and making sure we were focused. He created a really good atmosphere before the game. We weren't too intense, we weren't shouting or screaming, there was a very calm atmosphere and that was down to the manager.'

Something else that Strachan did that week was decide to bring a future Coventry captain into the squad for this huge match. A 17-year-old John Eustace travelled with the team, unsure of whether he would be named among the 16-strong matchday squad or not.

'I remember being on a pay phone at the hotel in the morning and Strachs walked past and asked if I was alright, and I said I was on the phone to my mum and dad,' he says. 'He said to tell them I was on the bench and that they should come to the game. I couldn't believe it, I was on the bench! They travelled up and just made the kick-off.'

Mr and Mrs Eustace were afforded slightly longer to make it to White Hart Lane due to a delayed kick-off. With traffic chaos on the M1, the match was delayed by 15 minutes, completely negating the entire point of all fixtures starting at the same time on the final day – and possibly giving City an advantage come the final minutes. That posed a problem for the man in the middle that day, veteran referee Martin Bodenham.

'There was a safety issue,' he explains, regarding the controversial delayed kick-off. 'The referees were told that all games had to kick off at 4pm. I think there was a problem with the turnstiles and they were worried about overcrowding. The police commissioner came to me before kick-off and said that we had to delay. I said, "We can't delay the kick-off." But obviously we had to. You're guided by the police, you can't override them. The police were aware that we wanted all of the games to start at the same time but safety comes first.'

But, with all this talk of 15-minute delays, we're getting ahead of ourselves. There were 75 minutes of on-field torture to endure before we got to that final quarter of an hour. In fact, even the 15-minute delay wasn't enough to ensure that Bryan Richardson made it on time.

'It was my youngest son's confirmation in Malvern so I was late getting to the match,' he says. 'I drove from Malvern to White Hart Lane and we scored while I was parking. I heard this roar and thought Tottenham had scored. I had put a box of champagne in the boot of the car because I had a feeling we would win. I didn't know what would happen with the other results, obviously. I thought, though, that if we won they deserved at least something out of it. Relegation was very much in my thinking. We would have had to sell players. But it wasn't as severe to get relegated then as it was in 2001 because we hadn't got players at that point on those big contracts.'

The chairman may have missed kick-off, but thousands of City fans reached White Hart Lane in time. These were fans who were owed a performance after the poor result the previous week, according to the seasoned shot-stopper Ogrizovic.

'We blew it by losing at home against Derby,' he says. 'We felt that we owed the fans, the club, everybody after that game. I look at all of the games I played in and the atmosphere and expectation of that Spurs game was incredible. I don't know if White Hart Lane was full but it felt full, it felt full of Coventry fans. The Coventry fans travelled in their thousands for this game. They believed that yet again we could survive.'

The match marked a return to White Hart Lane for Strachan just over two years after the night that he inspired City to a 3-1 win over the same hosts. Doing so had, of course, guaranteed survival in the 1994/95 season. He was, however, not in any great hurry to get his boots on for this one.

'Spurs was a decent ground for me but that was a strange day,' he says. 'I'd played in most of the games leading up to that and we'd had a good run, but we had the bad result against Derby. The stress against Tottenham was too much. I was a sub and Alex Miller wanted me to go on, Garry [Pendrey] wanted me to go on in the second half. I literally couldn't speak, never mind do a warm-up.'

City fielded a team with plenty of attacking intent, boasting Whelan, Ndlovu, Dublin and Huckerby alongside the assured heads of McAllister and Richardson further back in midfield. As was the case so many times down the years, it was the McAllister and Dublin partnership that proved vital. With just 13 minutes played Sky Blue nerves were somewhat settled as Dublin headed City in front. McAllister's corner was played back to him by Whelan, allowing the captain to find the head of Dublin with a pinpoint cross. City were one up. The late kick-off meant that the other two key matches were around the half-hour mark and both were still goalless. As things stood, City were safe. Six minutes before half-time City doubled their lead. Another assist came for McAllister as his cross was steered home from around the penalty spot by Paul Williams. But, just as it looked as if City could relax, Spurs grabbed a goal back a minute before the break. Teddy Sheringham's stinging 30-yard free kick clattered back off the woodwork and on to the head of Paul McVeigh, who nodded home. It was 2-1 at the break, and with both Sunderland and Middlesbrough still drawing their respective matches, Coventry were hanging in there.

The second half was a nervy affair for the Sky Blues, particularly when word filtered through that Sunderland had lost their match with Wimbledon 1-0 and Middlesbrough had been held 1-1 by Leeds. All City had to do was hang on, a win would see them safe, but a draw or defeat meant relegation. City's coaching staff were adamant that another experienced head was required on the pitch, but Strachan was having none of it.

'Alex Miller was at one end of the dugout, Garry Pendrey was at the other, so I sat in the middle where neither could speak to me,' Strachan recalls. 'Garry eventually said to me that Darren Huckerby was shattered and I needed to get on and just play off the front and slow the game down. I shouted to Darren, asking how he was, and he said he was shattered. Garry asked me what Darren said and I said, "He says he's fine!" I literally couldn't take my tracksuit bottoms off, I was that stressed.'

Strachan was instead keen to give the teenager on the bench a runout.

John Eustace says, 'With about five minutes to go the gaffer says to me, "John, get warmed up, you're going on." Garry Pendrey turned to him and said, "There's no effing chance he's going on now with five minutes to go, don't be so stupid." I didn't end up going on, I was relieved a little bit, in a funny way.'

There was relief all around soon enough, but not before Coventry's record appearance-holder Ogrizovic added to his already sizeable legacy with the club. With nerves jangling, Oggy pulled off several saves, including a superb block with his feet when Neale Fenn managed to lose Paul Williams and fire in a shot from eight yards.

'I made a big save and you have those big moments in games sometimes,' Ogrizovic says in particularly understated fashion. 'They are defining saves. Every single player on that day against Spurs was fantastic. We got our noses in front and deserved it. The second half, and the last 20 minutes in particular, we were coming under more and more pressure.'

Oggy's heroics provided the nerviest of moments in a nerve-shredding afternoon. Soon, the final whistle blew and City's players, fans and management celebrated with a mix of smiles and tears.

'That's a day I'll never forget,' says David Burrows. 'It was the first time I've ever shed tears on the pitch. It wasn't just the match, it was the build-up for weeks before. We knew what was at stake. None of us wanted to be the ones to take Coventry down, no one wanted that on their CV. We started 15 minutes late, it's these little things that happened during this period. It's never happened to me when a team has to wear the opposition team's shirt or it's the last day and everyone wants to kick off at the same time and one team kicks off 15 minutes later. We had the information, we knew what was going on. That made it even more intense, especially when Spurs scored. It was terrifying, I've never been so terrified on the pitch in all my life. We were just staring at the ref for about the last four minutes, just going, "Please just put that whistle in your mouth." I'm sure that game took years off my life [laughs]. It was euphoria to start but then we had to analyse what had gone wrong that season. Towards the end Oggy made some great saves.'

Strachan was also keen to point to the contribution of the veteran between the sticks.

'The performance was terrific,' he says. 'We were 2-1 up and then, arguably Coventry's greatest-ever player, Oggy, makes this fantastic save with his feet. We were 15 minutes behind everybody and that's why in that last 15 minutes I could hardly say a thing. It was a memorable day.'

For Oggy, the win was comparable with the club's finest hour.

'That feeling at the final whistle, it was as good as the FA Cup Final feeling a decade before,' he says. 'It was incredible that we had stayed up. A lot of players had their family in the stands. My wife, daughter and son were in the stand with the Coventry fans and the fans were brilliant because they helped get my children to the front so I could give them a hug. They were passing them down through the crowd because word had got around that they were my children.'

'It was a miraculous escape when we all thought we were down,' adds club historian Jim Brown. 'I thought we were down. The win at Anfield was amazing and we thought maybe we could do it. We beat Chelsea but then slipped up against Derby and we thought, "That's it." But then you know that if Sunderland ever get a whiff of relegation then they're going to go down!'

John Eustace points to the job Strachan did in the build-up to the match as key in City getting the result that they so desperately needed.

'We had nothing to lose,' he says. 'Everyone had said we were going to get relegated and the odds were against us so it was a relaxed week. I think that's why we performed so well. The build-up in the week was, "Look lads, you never know, it's highly unlikely because we need these other results to go our way but just go out there, enjoy it … it could be the last time you're in the Premier League but stranger things have happened." As the game went on the tension grew more and more because we knew things were going our way. It was buzzing afterwards. I remember on the bus back there were fans on the motorway bridges with banners out there. It was brilliant.'

For Dion Dublin the day was all about ensuring that his team did their job and hoping that would be enough.

'That was a horrible day,' he says. 'We knew we could beat anybody, we had good enough players but we were so inconsistent, that was our problem. We could beat anyone but we couldn't maintain a winning run. On that day we just said in the dressing room, "We just have to do our job. Let's do our job, give every ounce of energy, leave it all out there. Give blood and sweat, give everything and don't give them anything." I remember afterwards Gordon jumping on me like a koala with his legs wrapped around me.'

Liam Daish, who was injured that day and watched from the sidelines, recalls the coach stopping in Leamington on the way home and the squad piling out for an almighty celebration. Richard Shaw also remembers it being a night befitting such a huge day and he's adamant that the celebration was well deserved after securing another year at English football's top table.

'You can only imagine the scenes after the game,' he says. 'We were celebrating avoiding relegation, but at Coventry, being in the Premier League is a massive achievement. Staying in the Premier League was an incredible achievement. That really set us up for 97/98 as well.'

The Sky Blues survived by just one point, with Nottingham Forest, Middlesbrough and Sunderland the three teams to lose their top-flight status. Bizarrely, one point was also the gap between City down in 18th and Blackburn way up in 13th. In fact, if Strachan's men had turned two of their defeats into victories they would have finished in the top half of the table. Regardless, the key point was that survival had been assured and the club could now begin planning for another year in the Premier League.

Team	P	GD	Pts
17. Coventry	38	-18	41
18. Sunderland (R)	38	-18	40
19. Middlesbrough (R)	38	-9	39

Before focus could switch to the new season, there was one more match to be played. Over a year on from his career-ending injury, Dave Busst was set to finally benefit from a testimonial match. Fittingly, it was Manchester United who were due to visit Highfield Road for the occasion.

'When it was announced that I was retiring, someone asked Alex Ferguson if they would bring a team down and he said yes straightaway,' Busst recalls. 'There was a committee who arranged the testimonial. We beat Tottenham at the weekend to stay up and then on the Monday I had a phone call to say people were queuing up around the ground. I wondered what the bloody hell people were queuing for and it turned out it was for tickets for my benefit match. It ended up as a sell-out. That still sticks in my heart today; the support from the people of Coventry.'

The capacity crowd that witnessed the match on 16 May 1997 was treated to a real spectacle. A Sky Blues team turned out that featured Paul Gascoigne, Les Ferdinand and even Oggy playing outfield. For the opposition, the near full-strength team included Eric Cantona. The Frenchman announced his retirement days later, meaning that this was the final match in his truly incredible career. After the final whistle, Busst was pleased to receive an unexpected memento from the enigmatic striker.

'My uncle was on the organising committee,' he says. 'He didn't know much about football and he went into the Man United dressing room afterwards and asked for some shirts for me. My uncle said, "I don't know who signed this." It turned out it was Cantona's signed shirt!'

The match ended 2-2 with Busst scoring a last-minute penalty and, with that, the 1996/97 season was over. The 1997/98 season was coming, and what a year that was to prove to be, with records and hearts broken.

8.

Broken Records ... and Hearts

AFTER ANOTHER final-day escape the message was loud and clear – this could not happen again. To give the Sky Blues the best chance of not relying on last-minute heroics, the club's scouting network was used to the fullest throughout the 1997/98 season.

That didn't mean big money being thrown around, though. That summer's signings consisted of unknowns from the Continent and lower league talent. Strikers Kyle Lightbourne and Simon Haworth both fell into the latter category, joining in deals from Walsall and Cardiff, respectively, for £500,000 apiece. The same amount was spent on Trond Egil Soltvedt, an industrious midfielder brought in from Rosenborg. Soltvedt had impressed Ron Atkinson as part of the Rosenborg team that had beaten AC Milan in the Champions League the previous year.

'At that time Roma wanted to buy me and I had agreed that, but because we beat Milan we went in the quarter-final of the Champions League and Rosenborg refused to sell me,' says Soltvedt. 'We then played Juventus in the next round and I scored a goal and was the player of the match. The funny thing was that Ron Atkinson was working at the Champions League games. The previous year we had been in the same group as Blackburn so he had seen me in a couple of games and that's how the interest from Coventry came about.'

Soltvedt was invited to Ryton for the club to take a look at him, and for him to do the same to the club. He arrived with one vital part of a footballer's kit bag missing.

'I didn't take any boots with me and I went to the training ground to see what it was like,' he says. 'Gordon Strachan was there and he was brilliant with me. We were going to play Liverpool at Anfield the next day. He asked if I had any boots, I said no and he knew which boots I usually wore and the size and he had some for me and some kit so I could join in with training. We played an 11v11 to prepare for the game. David Burrows was back after a bad injury. It was a bit wet and I went into this tackle, and I was never afraid to go in for a tackle, and I smashed into Bugsy. When I went in, one of my feet slipped on the grass and went up under his knee. He went over the top of me right up in the air. I saw Strachan, he turned and said, "Woah!" I went to see that Bugsy was okay and he was screaming a little bit. I helped him up and he said, "Fucking great tackle!" After that I think Strachan knew that he wanted to bring me in.'

That magical £500,000 fee was also splashed on goalkeeper Magnus Hedman, from Swedish side AIK.

'I knew Coventry were looking at me, Bryan Richardson was watching me when AIK played Barcelona and I had a good game,' says Hedman. 'Then, we had a cup final in Sweden and Jim Blythe was there to watch me. Atlético Madrid and Espanyol also wanted me but the Premier League had always been a dream for me, so as soon as I heard about Coventry's interest there wasn't any question. Coventry was also a good-sized club for me, going abroad for the first time. The first day when I trained there I met with Graham Hover and he gave me a set of car keys and said the car was outside. I was so messed up because you guys drive on the other side of the road, so I had to sit and wait for other cars so I could follow them and drive on the correct side of the road!'

Hedman had just broken into the Swedish national team and many, himself included, presumed he would be fast-tracked into the starting line-up. But he found an immovable object in his way.

'It was quite tough in the beginning because I was just on my way into the Swedish national team, I had come from a very good season with AIK and then I met the wall of Steve Ogrizovic, a man who had been at the club for fucking decades!' he laughs. 'That was a tough task. Even then, I never complained, I just trained as hard as I could and pushed Oggy. I wanted to be a proper team-mate. I knew I couldn't go up to the gaffer and complain. It was a tough couple of months for me to be on the bench. I hadn't come to just sit on the bench but I don't like this thing in football where someone is certain to play. The best player for the day is the one that should play. It was a new league for me so maybe Strachan wanted me to get a feel for everything before he gave me the chance. I was living my dream by playing in the Premier League with Coventry.'

Soltvedt was also having a few issues in settling in. For him, it wasn't finding his place in the team that was the immediate concern, instead it was understanding his new manager.

'My English was not the best back then and with Strachan and his Scottish dialect it was not easy to understand him always,' he admits. 'I had to learn English the hard way, through Gordon Strachan. The funny thing was that in the second season Dion would ask me, "Trond, what is he saying? What is he saying?" He was asking me because Strach spent loads of time with me. Every Monday we had a session with five against five and Strach would always pick me in his team. Dion would call me Strach's son and when it was time to pick the teams he would say, "Trond, just go to your dad."'

The Norwegian midfielder was as fit as they come and able to cover ground from first whistle to last. But, much to his surprise, he found there were a couple of workhorses already at the club that had the beating of him in the fitness stakes.

'The pre-season in Coventry, especially the first season, it was the hardest of my life,' he says. '[Strachan] was a nutter, he would run us hard but when we got into the season we were so fit. Through the season he worked us quite hard but then when it came to Thursday he would slow down a little bit ahead of the game. I've never been in a better shape than I was in that time. I was a strong runner in Norway and held some of the records. I was one of the best testers with running. Then I got to Coventry and I couldn't catch Noel Whelan and Paul Telfer, fucking hell they were strong runners, they were two nutters. I was always used to being the man who was first and all of a sudden there were these two ahead of me.'

Roland Nilsson was the other notable summer signing, joining for £200,000. Those unfamiliar with the full-back's work may have been underwhelmed by the signing of a 33-year-old, but the Sweden international quickly did his talking on the pitch, proving himself to be an incredibly consistent athlete and one of the classiest players to ever don the sky blue jersey. It's telling that whenever Nilsson's name cropped up in conversation with any of his team-mates interviewed for this book, they without exception added 'a Rolls-Royce of a player' immediately after saying his name.

As well as the arrivals, there was the departure of a huge fan favourite from the club's Premier League journey. In his pomp, Peter Ndlovu had been linked with many of the country's top teams, particularly Liverpool, but when he finally made the move away from Coventry in the summer of 1997, it was down to the second tier in a transfer to Birmingham. In the course of conducting interviews for this book, the fact that Ndlovu didn't make the move to a club battling at the top of the table was a surprise to many.

'He shouldn't have been playing for Birmingham,' says Ron Atkinson. 'If it had been earlier on, I'd have taken him when I was at Man United. He was an absolute player. He was brilliant. I never had an offer for Nuddy while I was there.'

'That is a big statement,' Ndlovu says in response to Ron's above comment. 'That is great for these people who have mastered football to speak like that about me, just an African boy who came to England. I wish Ron had seen me back then so I could have signed for Manchester! I respect Coventry so much though, because that is where I made my name. Coventry gave me a platform to perform at the highest level. Playing for Coventry was a highlight of my career. I really appreciate being thought of as a legend there. It makes me so proud. Playing for Coventry was just a joy for me. The club means a lot to me.'

'I love Peter,' John Salako adds. 'He was so talented, so amazing, two-footed, with balance and grace. I just couldn't believe he didn't get the chance to play for a top club. He could have played for anyone. We were so lucky to have him.'

Bryan Richardson admits that the much-rumoured moves to Liverpool and Spurs were never in the pipeline for Ndlovu.

'We never, ever once had a sniff of anyone wanting to sign Ndlovu,' he says. 'I kept reading in the papers that these teams were looking at him and he was top of their list but we never had a single show of interest from one of the bigger clubs for him. In the end he was struggling because of his knees and we did a deal with Birmingham, which was £1m plus £200,000 every 20 games up to another £1m.'

While not yet the financial force that they would soon become, opening-day visitors to Highfield Road Chelsea were fancied by many for a title charge under Ruud Gullit and would represent a stern test for City. It's fair to say that the visitors arrived in Coventry feeling pretty confident.

'When Chelsea came to town to play us on the opening day of the season they bowled in,' recalls Dion Dublin. 'We were in the dressing room and Strachan was the last person to come into the dressing room on the day. Strachan had seen the Chelsea coach turn up and he saw how they got off the coach. They had their baseball caps on backwards, tracksuit bottoms up, one player was on the fitness coach's back. They were just peeing about. They weren't taking us or Highfield Road seriously. What Strachan did was he got to us quickly, he ran down and opened our double doors and told us he wanted us to look at the door. We saw every Chelsea player walking by all jovial, not taking us seriously. Strachan shut the door and said, "They don't have an ounce of respect for you lads, not one ounce and this is your home. This is your house." We went out and stuffed them.'

In fairness to the visitors, they started well and took the lead through Frank Sinclair. Two minutes later, a near-post Dublin header levelled the scores and just a minute later Dublin struck again at the near post to put City ahead at the break. Chelsea restored parity midway through the second half but Dublin completed his hat-trick and sealed the points with a beautiful left-foot control, right-foot finish with just two minutes left. It was the second time within a few months that Chelsea had come to town and been unable to handle Coventry's attacking threat. At least they remembered their kit this time.

'Huck would terrorise Chelsea,' says Strachan. 'We told Huck to just stand beside Leboeuf when we were defending and when we got the ball to just run off him. That was our tactic. We could play any sort of game. We could chip the ball up to Dion. There's a big difference between chipping the ball up to his head, chest or feet and playing a long ball. It's a long pass. When Glenn Hoddle hits one it's a long pass. When Liam Daish did it people said it was a long hoof. They're the same thing. Dion could bring it under control and bring people into play. If people pushed up on you, Darren could run in behind. If he came short and turned on people he could drive at teams. We worked on that a lot. It wasn't cosmic coaching, it was just common sense.'

Huckerby relished the task of making a World Cup winner look like a Sunday League clogger.

'Lebouef and Desailly were World Cup winners but I just found that Lebouef couldn't handle me,' he says. 'Not in one-on-one situations, I was too quick for him. When you've got Dion holding the ball up, flicking things on and putting you in, it's a big help. Teams just couldn't handle us, especially that season.'

It was to be an exciting campaign, but the inconsistency that followed suggested it could be another tough year. A home fixture with Bolton three matches into the season summed up the stuttering start. City led 2-0 and looked to be cruising before Peter Beardsley inspired a Bolton comeback and it ended 2-2. September, meanwhile, saw a run of just one goal in six matches, with some light relief saved for the League Cup as Everton were thrashed 4-1. The club's long-held tradition of gifting the league's basket case three points continued with Barnsley the latest benefactors in a 2-0 defeat as the Sky Blues ended October with just two wins in the first 12 league matches.

A win over Wimbledon followed but defeats returned thick and fast with three local derby losses in a row against Derby, Leicester and Aston Villa. After 17 matches of the season, the Sky Blues had just three wins and, while not quite down in the bottom three, were mired in the bottom third of the table. To make matters worse, captain and midfield driving engine Gary McAllister was stretchered off in the Leicester match with a knee injury. Reluctant to undergo surgery that would rule him out of the rest of the season and the 1998 World Cup, McAllister missed just one match before returning to the team. He was back against Spurs at Highfield Road but lasted only 31 minutes before being forced off. He would undergo cruciate ligament surgery and not play again until the following October. In his absence, the team smashed Spurs in an emphatic 4-0 win.

'Dion and Darren were terrorising defenders that season,' recalls Marcus Hall. 'We had a 4-0 against Tottenham and it was fantastic for me to get a goal in that one. I mean, I know it was the fourth one and they were probably on their heels by that point!'

The long-term loss of McAllister was a huge concern, not helped by the back-to-back defeats that followed. Soltvedt had been a regular alongside McAllister, and European scout Ray Clarke would deliver an early Christmas present to the club by unearthing the man that would take the skipper's place for much of the remainder of the season. A swashbuckling Dutch right-back by the name of George Boateng signed on 18 December in a £220,000 deal.

Clarke had come to the club's attention after being sent on a scouting mission while working for Graeme Souness at Southampton. The Saints boss tasked Clarke with running the rule over Peter Ndlovu but Souness was sacked soon after, a move that resulted in Clarke also losing his job. A link-up with Coventry followed and Clarke was given the job of scouting in Europe, predominantly Belgium and the Netherlands. Such was his commitment to the role, he ended up moving to the Netherlands, where he witnessed all kinds of gems coming through, with a 16-year-old Arjen Robben among those catching his eye. One of his finds that made their way to Coventry was Boateng.

'He was playing right-back or left-back,' he recalls. 'My words to Gordon and Bryan were that if he wasn't quite the ticket, he would at least be a good squad player who could play right-back, left-back and in midfield. He settled in the middle of the park. I used to watch him at Feyenoord and you could see his intensity. That intensity made me think he could play in England. We know that in Holland they have great technical players but sometimes they can't deal with the intensity of the game. I felt that he could. He was after people, getting his foot in, closing them down.

In English football, if you can do that then you're going to be successful.'

Boateng could have been joined in Coventry by an attacking midfielder who became a hero at Arsenal not long after.

'The one I kept rattling Bryan's cage about was Freddie Ljungberg,' Clarke says. 'I put him under his nose four or five times. He's one that we could have got because Arsenal only paid £3m for him. Now I'm not saying we could pay £3m but he would be the one that we should have gone and got.'

Nonetheless, Boateng was signed and made his debut five days before Christmas 1997 in a 1-0 loss against Liverpool.

'We were looking at him, thinking, "Oh my god, what a player!"' says Richard Shaw. 'Trond as well, he wasn't a George but he was a destroyer and he would block passing lines. I loved Trond. That season was built on our recruitment.'

The industrious midfield duo of Boateng and Soltvedt quickly clicked, aided by the attacking talents of Noel Whelan, with Dublin and Huckerby further forward.

'We were workhorses together,' Soltvedt says of his midfield partner. 'We may not have been the best all of the time but we gave everything. That was the thing with Gordon Strachan, we worked hard.'

While things hadn't quite clicked in terms of results, that was about to change as two of the most memorable wins of Coventry's decade came within days of each other. Three days after Christmas, Manchester United were the visitors and Gordon Strachan met his team with a forthright message ahead of kick-off.

'Before the Man United game Strachan said to us, "No one is here to watch you, they're all here to watch Beckham, Giggs and so on, so just go out and enjoy it,"' says Magnus Hedman, who was in the midst of his first extended run in the team.

The Sky Blues trailed 2-1 in the final stages, having led through a Noel Whelan goal in the first half. With just four minutes left it became the Darren Huckerby show. First, he won a penalty, which Dublin converted for the equaliser, and then with 88 minutes on the clock he ran from the halfway line, slalomed his way through the United defence and finished past Kevin Pilkington for surely the finest goal of his career.

'That goal gets remembered,' he says. 'Beating Man United in the last minute when Man United were Man United, not this sorry state that they are now, was special. Back then, with the players that they had, to get any kind of result against Man United was very, very difficult unless you were a top two or three team. We deserved to win that. Sometimes you nick a lucky 1-0 win where everything goes for you but we created some chances, quite a few chances. Even now, 25 years later, I must get it sent to me on Twitter 50 times a year, and I re-tweet every single one! Some Coventry fans say it's the greatest moment they've ever had. That's so nice. For a club over 100 years old and for some people that's their best moment, you've got to be happy with that.'

Huckerby had every right to be happy a few days later as Coventry travelled to Anfield for the third round of the FA Cup. Liverpool took the lead but were then completely outplayed by a rampant Sky Blues team. There was no magical plan that was tailored just to this match; it was just this Coventry team doing what they did best through the tireless work rate of the defence and midfield and the constant attacking threat carried by Huckerby and Dublin.

'We weren't given a chance,' admits Marcus Hall. 'Everyone expected us to go to Liverpool, lose and go out in the third round and that was the cup run over. We went to Anfield and didn't do anything different, we just went with the determination to win the game. Strachan never set us up to do anything other than try to win the game.'

The Sky Blues ran out 3-1 winners thanks to goals from Huckerby, Dublin and Telfer. Strachan pinpoints that man Huckerby as key to the victory.

'Huckerby was coming in from the left-hand side and taking shots,' he says. 'He was terrorising people. He had these days where he was absolutely unplayable. It was great because we never had a clue what he was doing so the other team definitely had no clue what he was going to do! He was one of those players.'

'To go to Anfield is hard but we absolutely battered Liverpool that day,' Huckerby adds. 'They had some really good players, like McManaman, Fowler, Owen, and were a really good Premier League team and we absolutely smashed them. We were on a run where anything was possible.'

David Burrows enjoyed a career at a host of top clubs, yet he singles this match out for some special praise.

'This was one of our best-ever performances,' he says. 'We absolutely destroyed Liverpool. Huckerby was outstanding. That was one of my favourite days from my entire career.'

Dublin and Huckerby had once again clicked into gear and looked a formidable partnership, especially with Whelan supporting from midfield. Coventry started 1998 down in 14th place, but this attacking trio would inspire a rise up the table. They hit a 13-match spell around the turn of the year in which they scored 20 goals between them. Not bad considering the entire team only managed 38 goals in the 38 league matches of the previous season. With the attacking talent working so well together, what happened next came as a surprise. Summer signings Haworth and Lightbourne had struggled for goals, and for opportunities in the team to be fair, and both would be shipped out before long. To bolster the attacking options, Strachan splashed a club record £3.25m fee on Romanian striker Viorel Moldovan. Coventry aren't the kind of club to spend that much on a squad player, but Dublin and Huckerby weren't ones to give up their places in the team without a fight.

'Viorel Moldovan – get yourself on the bench, son, get yourself on the bench!' laughs Dublin. '[Seeing him come in] made us play better. It puts you on hot coals seeing someone come in who could take your place; he wanted my shirt. The signing of Moldovan was a sign of progression that we wanted to make the team better. It was a positive move to get him in, he had scored a lot of goals and a lot for Romania. He was a potent goalscorer but we were playing so well that he couldn't get into the side.'

It was a signing that Huckerby failed to see the thinking behind.

'Moldovan was a strange signing,' he says. 'I never understood it even when he arrived. I didn't understand why he was there. We had three forwards who were good enough to play week in, week out and we bought a fourth one who didn't really fit into our style of play. There's no doubt he was a good player. He had an international pedigree and I think he was a really good finisher. He was completely different from myself, Dion and Noel Whelan but he didn't really suit how we played.'

There were also suggestions that Moldovan, who arrived with a very limited grasp of English, didn't see eye to eye with some of his team-mates.

'There was a clash of personalities between Huckerby and Moldovan,' says Andy Turner. 'One time at the training ground there was a big kerfuffle because in the corridors at Ryton they had blown-up photographs that the *Coventry Telegraph* photographers had taken. They were all down the corridor. There was one of Moldovan on the wall and someone had defaced it with a comedy moustache, googly eyes or whatever with a marker pen. It was suggested that Huckerby had done it. Moldovan was a bit upset about it and thought it was disrespectful.'

Strachan echoes Dublin's earlier comments that the mere arrival of Moldovan kept the club's existing strikers on their toes.

'We bought Moldovan but the strikers that we had saw him off,' he says. 'He was a good player. What happens when you bring good players in is that the ones that are already there think, "Hang on a minute, we need to up our game." It's unfortunate for the player coming in because he was a goalscorer and he came in to fight for a place but [Dublin and Huckerby] were absolutely on fire.'

Richard Shaw reckons adding depth to the squad was nothing new.

'Competition is a good thing,' he says. 'Strachs used to buy a new centre-half every year. Me and Willo would say, "Are you taking the piss?!" It kept us on our toes. Dion, Hucks and Whelan were as good a front three as I saw. If you put that front three in the Man United team, it wouldn't change Man United, that's how good they were. Buying Moldovan just gave those three a kick up the backside.'

That fantastic Liverpool victory in the third round was followed by a fourth-round win against Derby, a team that City had struggled to find the measure of in recent years. That win started what would become a record-breaking run of victories that stretched from late January to early March. Highlights included a 5-1 tonking of Bolton in which Dublin, Huckerby and Whelan put on an absolute masterclass in attacking play. Dublin and Huckerby were both receiving plenty of plaudits, the former earning the Premier League Player of the Month award for February and his first England cap in a friendly against Chile on 11 February.

'Getting the England call-up was incredible,' Dublin says. 'It's one of those calls that you hope through all your career that you will get. You keep your head down and keep scoring goals then you become hard to ignore. Glenn [Hoddle] liked me as a footballer. When I got the call it was special. I was jumping around the lounge and then was straight on the phone to my family. I might have had a few beers that night!'

The Huckerby–Dublin partnership was so good that they convinced Strachan to turn down the chance to sign a future Premier League golden boot winner.

'I went out to watch Ruud van Nistelrooy while he was at Heerenveen,' Strachan says. 'He was going to cost about £6m and I was thinking who would I leave out, because I had Dion and Huckerby and they were on fire. To spend that kind of money we had to guarantee they would be better than those two. To be fair, when we found out the other teams who were in for him we realised it was perhaps a wasted journey. But those two were so good that we were wondering whether it was worth bringing this lad in.'

Not a bad endorsement for Dublin and Huckerby, right? Never mind Moldovan, even Van Nistelrooy couldn't get them out of the team! Outside of Coventry, these two don't get mentioned enough when the usual suspects of Yorke and Cole, Shearer and Sheringham et al are spoken of as the best strike duos of the 90s.

'When Hucks turned up it just seemed to click,' says Dublin. 'We were close and we still are today. We hit it off. I probably took all of the heavyweight hits and Hucks did all of the running in behind. That's what he was good at, he was one of the fastest things on two legs I've ever seen. We worked on it a lot in training. People knew exactly where I would be if they were on the wing, if Hucks was on the wing, everyone would know where we both would be and how to play it. We were a partnership and, I don't know how, but telepathically we just knew where each other would be. I wouldn't have got into the England side without Hucks. No chance.'

Huckerby is quick to acknowledge that, while there was unmistakable chemistry between himself and Dublin, plenty of work also went into the partnership.

'It's all about what goes on behind the scenes,' he says. 'Back then in the afternoons me and Dion would be out working with the kids on different things. Me being a young lad, I was wondering why I was there in the afternoon. We were flying, everyone else had gone home and there was me, Dion and Noel Whelan working on bits and bobs with

Gordon. When you get older you realise he was doing that to make us all a better player. Not necessarily to make the club better, to make individual players better. I've played for probably 15 managers and I can name one or two who cared if the players got better or not. Gordon cared. All managers care if the team does well on a Saturday but they're not bothered if the players get better. Gordon cared about that. All of the players at the club at that time bought into it.'

This notion of everyone buying into what was going on helped to nurture an incredible team spirit in the dressing room. Team spirit cropped up again and again during interviews and one man who was there for almost all of the Premier League era sees this particular squad as having a special bond.

'You can't be successful in any team sport without a level of togetherness and team spirit,' Steve Ogrizovic says. 'The players not in the side are sometimes as important as the players in the side. I've experienced both ends. I've been in good dressing rooms with positive characters, players who socialise off the pitch. A sports scientist can't measure team spirit. You can't measure what a good night out does to a dressing room. Team spirit got us over the line as early as 1985 when we stayed up, and again in 1987 at Wembley. The other time I really encountered a fantastic team spirit was 1996 to 1999 at Coventry. That team really gelled and you could feel that in the changing room.'

'We had some great times, big characters; that dressing room was hardcore,' Dublin adds. 'There was a lot of leaders, lots of captains and we looked after each other. We had a lot of players who were happy to take responsibility. That is very rare, especially nowadays. With that squad, if something wasn't right, we would possibly put it right on the pitch without even asking the manager. We would have a conversation during a corner or a free kick and pull each other in. We wouldn't allow each other to get a free ride and we would hold each other accountable for our actions. If your man gets a free header from a corner and scores, you're going to get dog's abuse. You have to pull your weight because we weren't good enough to carry people. People like Willo, Shaw, myself, Gary Mac, Roland Nilsson, Paul Telfer, we would all be telling people that they had to pull their weight.'

One of the bigger characters in the dressing room also stresses the importance of the togetherness that united this Coventry squad.

'I'd take character over talent all day long,' says Noel Whelan. 'We were tight on and off the field. I had my own home but I generally lived with Paul Telfer the majority of the time. At the end of every season, six or seven of us would go away together to Ayia Napa and spend a week together even after being together every day for the whole season. You've got to have characters in the dressing room. My character was probably a little bit different to most people's [laughs]. But they all found good fun in whatever mistakes I made and whatever I was up to. I was always a talking point in the changing room. There was never a dull moment when I was about, I think most of the players would agree with that. I think most of them would say I was mental more than anything. That was just me, I was energetic, boisterous, playful at times. Some things that I did were across the line, obviously, but I never hurt anyone but myself. If there were ever any problems outside a ground or when we went out I'd always be the one to look after certain people. I guess that was my downfall. I'd protect people when I needed to and I got the brunt of it.'

* * *

The Sky Blues were flying in the league and picked up five wins on the spin, seven in a row in all competitions. The most memorable of these came on Valentine's Day 1998 as City faced Aston Villa at Villa Park in the FA Cup. To say the club's record at this particular venue was poor is an understatement, with not a single win in the last 26 attempts. But something was special about this season.

City rocked up at Villa Park and did the unthinkable – they won! It was that man Moldovan who got the only goal of the match. The Romanian had been almost shoe-horned into the team in recent weeks, with Dublin moving back to centre-half to accommodate him. The move paid off this day, as the record signing was on hand to tap in the loose ball after a superb George Boateng run and shot had been parried away. The team sheet that day also included the full debut of Gordon's son Gavin.

'Afterwards Oggy said to me he'd been going to Villa Park for years and never won and then I go and do it on my debut!' he says. 'As a young lad I thought it would be like that all of the time. I didn't realise what a big deal it was.'

'It was about 100 years since we'd won at Villa Park!' Strachan senior adds. 'You knew it was a special day. All of the build-up was that Coventry just didn't win at Villa Park. We had a few injuries because Gavin made his debut that day. That was all down to Gary McAllister. As a dad you're overprotective and you're also thinking a couple of years ago it seemed a good idea to sign your son but now you worry if you pick him people will think it's nepotism. But Gary said, "He needs to play now." At the end of the game everyone was jumping about and he just got dressed and never said a thing. He just took it in. That's what happens when you're the son of the manager, you don't want to overreact. That was a special day.'

That aforementioned team spirit came back to the fore afterwards as many players headed out for a celebration but perhaps their choice of venue needed a little more thought.

'I'll tell you how confident we were, we beat Villa 1-0 at Villa Park and then we went out in Birmingham that night,' says Richard Shaw. 'That was probably the biggest mistake we made because we were told by some Villa fans in a bar in

no uncertain terms to get out! It was always great to beat the
Villa, especially at Villa Park.'

We had a highly rated coach in charge and were through
to the quarter-final of the FA Cup, while on a record-breaking
run of wins. Our centre-forward was playing for England.
We were dreaming, perhaps getting carried away with what
could come next.

'The Villa win was a bit like the win at Old Trafford in
the fourth round in 1987,' says Rob Gurney. 'Back then you
started to think it wasn't out of the question, and the Villa
win, because of the circumstances, you began to think it would
lead to something similar.'

In the league City had hit the top half, climbing as
high as ninth in February and with an eye on a charge for a
European place. Despite this excitement, the focus was on
the FA Cup. We had been given what looked a dream draw
in the quarter-final, at home to second tier Sheffield United.
Many of the big hitters had already been eliminated and
you could have made a decent argument that the Sky Blues
would have been favourites to come out on top against just
about any of the teams left in the competition, except for
Arsenal. The belief that a trip to Wembley *could* be on the
way was being replaced with an expectation that the club
would do it.

'The fans definitely thought we could get to Wembley,'
Ogrizovic, who was back in the team at this point, recalls.
'I don't think we thought our name was on the cup in 1987,
I think that's something that you think in hindsight. It's a
cliché, but as a player you're focused on one step at a time, one
game at a time. It was a difficult game, they were a division
below so it was one of those games where we were expected
to get through.'

Things started so well. Sheffield United were in turmoil,
going into the match managerless and were a goal down just
after the half-hour mark when Dublin converted a penalty.

Unfortunately, the Blades fought back and earned a 1-1 draw, forcing a replay at Bramall Lane ten days later.

'There was an air of, not arrogance, it was confidence,' David Burrows says. 'We'd drawn Sheffield United and saw a chance of reaching the semis. We underperformed. It was hugely disappointing that we didn't beat them at Highfield Road, we put in a poor performance on the day. Sheffield United had done their homework, fair play to them.'

It was a similar story in the replay as the Sky Blues again took the lead, this time through Telfer. With just seconds to go, a place in the semi-final was beckoning, until the most uncharacteristic of mistakes from our very own Mr Perfect.

'We were 1-0 up and with a minute or so to go Roland Nilsson, one of our most technically gifted players, an unbelievable player, the ball rolled towards him and it just hit the bottom of his studs with the faintest of touches so what could have been a goal kick ended up being a corner,' Ogrizovic recalls.

The resulting corner led to David Holdsworth levelling the scores with an acrobatic strike.

'David is a mate of mine and we spoke many times about this match,' says Burrows. 'He said they won that match at Highfield Road, without a shadow of a doubt, because getting us back to Bramall Lane, they were confident. For Holdsworth to score that volley, he'd never done it before and he never did it afterwards. I used to room with him afterwards at Birmingham and I'd say to him in training, "Go on, put a volley in like you did in the cup that night!" He just stuck his leg at it and it flew into the top corner.'

For Strachan, the final moments of the 90 minutes provided him with an unwanted memory that he carried for the rest of his career.

'We've taken a free kick and if we had put it into the corner then we're through to the semi-final,' he says. 'It's one of those things that you think is common sense but, no, we played it down the middle. Maybe as a manager I should have been emphasising to play it into the corner and if they headed it out we'd get a throw. That's one of those things that will always haunt you as a manager. I've got two or three of those stuck away in my locker.'

With that, the belief seemed to be drained out of the team. It was still all square after 120 minutes and the tie went to penalties. A couple of players who had experience of penalty-taking, Soltvedt and Moldovan, had both been subbed off during extra time, and the Norwegian is confident he would have stepped up had he been on the pitch.

'It's easy to say with hindsight but I was always on penalties,' he says. 'In Norway I took lots of penalties and in shoot-outs I always took penalties. I've never been afraid of taking a penalty. When you've been to the San Siro and beaten Milan you are mature and have no problem in taking a penalty.'

The shoot-out makes painful viewing even 25 years later. City actually grabbed an early advantage with Oggy saving the first penalty. Dublin, who had been first-choice taker in the absence of McAllister, went first for City and saw his effort saved by Alan Kelly. From there, United seized the advantage and didn't look back. Telfer converted his but Burrows and Haworth struck, in all honesty, weak penalties as Coventry crashed out 3-1 on spot kicks.

'Along with relegation, that night was my bitterest memory of following City in those years,' says Rob Gurney. 'Simon Haworth ends up taking a penalty. You wonder why on earth a 20-year-old reserve striker was taking a penalty. I didn't think that was fair on Haworth. Roland Nilsson was one that I couldn't understand why he didn't take one.'

It seems the decision to take such a vital kick was somewhat thrust upon Haworth.

'The disappointing thing for me was there were a few senior players who wouldn't take penalties,' he says. 'A few

149

players went missing. Strachs turned to me and said, "You'll take one, won't you?" I said, "Yeah, okay." I changed my mind several times before taking it and hit an absolute nothing of a penalty. I was thrown in at the deep end. Strachs asked me and I was never going to say no. We had some good, experienced players on there who didn't want to take one of the five penalties.'

I was 12 years old at this time. I still remember going to bed in floods of tears, distraught that we had blown the chance of Wembley. I thought to myself there was no way my mum would wake me up for school in the morning. After such a traumatic evening it would surely be best that I slept it off. I can confirm that I was in school bang on time the following day.

After such a deflating defeat you may have forgiven the season for petering out from there, but in fact some decent results were still to come. A spot in the UEFA Cup was still on the table for whoever finished seventh, and a win over Derby left City still in with a shout as we went into April.

Team	P	GD	Pts
7. Derby	30	+4	45
8. West Ham	29	+3	44
9. Coventry	30	+1	43

Next up was Leicester. The Sky Blues went into the match ninth in the table and in the mix for a European spot with the likes of Leicester, Derby, Villa and Blackburn. City only managed a draw with the Foxes and then lost against Villa.

Coventry ended the season with six matches unbeaten, but five of those were draws. A thrilling 3-3 with Leeds in which Huckerby bagged a hat-trick was a highlight, while a win came against Blackburn. Despite the draws, you can't say that Strachan's men had downed tools, as battling points were earned by coming from behind against Liverpool and Spurs.

The final day saw a bit of a novelty, a last-day relegation scrap where Coventry weren't under any pressure. City travelled to Goodison, with Everton needing a result to avoid the drop. It ended 1-1 thanks to a late Dublin header, his 18th goal of the season to give him a share of the golden boot. Both he and Huckerby had enjoyed the goalscoring seasons of their careers, with the latter weighing in with 14 league goals. The point was enough for Everton to survive. It wasn't enough for Coventry to sneak that European place, though – instead it went to Villa, of all teams. City ended up just outside the top half in 11th. The fine margins are shown by the fact that had the Sky Blues beaten Leicester rather than picking up a draw at the tail-end of the campaign, they would have finished above the Foxes and in the top half.

'We finished 11th and we should have got to a cup final,' says Huckerby. 'In a one-off game we were good enough to beat anybody. I'm not saying we would have won it but on our day we could beat anybody. Sheffield United in the quarters should have been a gimme, really.'

Team	P	GD	Pts
7. Aston Villa	38	+1	57
8. West Ham	38	-1	56
9. Derby	38	+3	55
10. Leicester	38	+10	53
11. Coventry	38	+2	52

Yes, there were some regrets, but given that Coventry only stayed up by the skin of their teeth the season before, this was a definite success of a campaign. It had seen some of the best football played at Highfield Road for many years and City had the hottest striking partnership in the country.

'After 97, when you look at 98, we played some of the most entertaining football that Coventry have ever experienced,' says Ogrizovic. 'It was a wonderful period.'

Before we sign off and move on to 1998/99, we should address a major elephant in the room. The issue of the sale of Highfield Road and the debacle that has followed the club regarding the ground in the decades since looms large over every aspect of Coventry City. As the club didn't leave Highfield Road until after the period covered by this book, I've chosen not to focus on it. Also, these issues have been covered, very well and at length, elsewhere already. But I must acknowledge that around this time the move away from Highfield Road was being planned. I'll leave the sole word on the issue to a man who, above all else, has been there, seen it and done it when it comes to Coventry City.

'In hindsight, the club was at that time probably trying to get a little bigger than it should have done, mainly with the talk of moving ground,' says record appearance holder Ogrizovic. 'In my experience, Highfield Road was perfect for the club; it was a fantastic ground, a great atmosphere, every team that came there felt under the cosh. For an old ground, it was actually quite modern as well because so much of it had been redeveloped. Highfield Road epitomised what Coventry City is about. New players were coming in, the Premier League money was there and we got too far ahead of ourselves with the intent of leaving Highfield Road and that was the start of the downfall.'

It wasn't evident just yet that we were on the downfall, but 1998/99 would bring mass disruption, never-ending contract negotiations, sales that would taint legacies for years to come and the departure of some of our most loved players.

9.

Dion Departs

AFTER THE red-hot form of Dublin and Huckerby the previous year, there was optimism for what 1998/99 had in store for the Sky Blues. In hindsight, this would have been the ideal time to strengthen with some extra quality, perhaps reinforcing the defence. Instead, the departures were more eye-catching in the summer of 1998 than the arrivals.

Viorel Moldovan, signed the previous year for £3.25m, left for Fenerbahçe for £4m, having failed to dislodge Dublin or Huckerby in attack. John Salako, an early Ron Atkinson signing, also moved on, leaving for Fulham on a free.

'Leaving was ridiculous,' Salako says of his departure. 'I don't think Strach thought I wanted to sign a contract. They wanted to give me a more incentivised pay-as-you-play contract and we weren't far away on it. I think Strach thought I didn't want to sign it and he's a fiery character and he just thought, "Sod you." We really should have sat down and signed another contract. I was gutted that I left, I'd have loved to have stayed another two or three years.'

Paul Hall, a £300,000 buy from Portsmouth, did little to raise excitement, but the arrival of Croatian international Robert Jarni certainly did. The cultured full-back was a real coup in a £2.6m switch from Real Betis. Unfortunately, the move was to be infamously short-lived. Just two weeks after the transfer, Jarni was off to Real Madrid. Rumours have long circled that the deal was the subject of a gentlemen's agreement to remedy Betis's refusal to sell directly to Madrid. Bryan Richardson refutes such claims, saying he and Strachan had been to watch Jarni play several times. When they made the decision to pull the trigger on the signing, Richardson was faced with the task of negotiating with Betis's notorious chairman, Manuel Ruiz de Lopera.

'The chairman of Betis was called the most evil man in Spain and I can believe that!' Richardson says. 'He was a tiny little chap and he sat on this plinth and this plinth was surrounded as if it were a chapel with crucifixes and pictures of the Virgin Mary. It was extraordinary. I didn't speak Spanish and he didn't speak English, so I had a guy with me who was bilingual. We sat there from 10am to 1pm and never once did he offer us even a glass of water. We broke for lunch and went back in from 2pm to 4.30pm, same again, nothing at all from him. When the deal was eventually done two and a half days later, he said, "Right, we now go for lunch," and we went to this fantastic restaurant and he bought lunch for everybody.'

With the deal done, Jarni travelled to Coventry with Richardson as the Sky Blues prepared for a pre-season tie with Espanyol. Jarni watched from the directors' box, but it quickly became evident that something wasn't right with the club's high-profile new signing.

'He was in the directors' box with his agent and I noticed he was on the phone a lot,' says Richardson. 'At half-time I asked the agent what the matter was. He said everything was fine and he was just talking to his wife. The next thing I hear is the agent comes and says there is a problem. Lorenzo Sanz, the president of Real Madrid, wanted Jarni to play for them and he had been talking to Robert's wife. She didn't want to leave Spain. The Betis man hears this and gets hold of me and said we hadn't completed on the deal. I told him we had, he was registered with us and we had paid the initial payment. He said he was returning the payment. I told him he couldn't do that, it was all done and we would pay him the other half of the deal now. He said, "No, I don't want it, I want Jarni back." I told him it was too late. We then had Lorenzo's recruitment guy on the phone and I told him they'd have to get here and we'd sort something out.'

The Sky Blues ended up bagging an £800,000 profit for a player who was with the club for just a fortnight as he moved on to Real Madrid for £3.4m. It was very nearly £3.5m, but lady luck deserted Richardson at the wrong moment.

'I tried to get £3.5m and we ended up tossing a coin for [the extra £100,000],' he says. 'They said no and I said I'd toss a coin for it. I talked them into doing that. We tossed a coin and unfortunately I lost.'

An international-quality defender had slipped through the club's fingers, but it left Strachan with a priceless piece of memorabilia.

'My strips all go away, I don't have any football memorabilia up in the house,' says Strachan. 'I was doing something the other day and found all of these strips and we found Robert Jarni's Coventry strip. That must be valuable!'

As Jarni sealed his switch to Madrid, the Sky Blues faced Chelsea on the opening day of the season. It was a repeat of the previous year's curtain-raiser and, when it came to the result, it was the same old story as the unfancied Sky Blues stole a march on the megabucks Londoners. Magnus Hedman began the season in goal and had by now established himself as number one, with club legend Steve Ogrizovic the understudy. The two had different approaches to the position. Understandably for a man a decade younger, Hedman was more of an athlete than Oggy and more comfortable with distribution. The Swede did, however, learn plenty from Oggy's vocal command of his defence.

'I studied Oggy quite a lot,' Hedman says. 'The main thing as a goalkeeper is you need to be good at communication, that is number one. It's not just about talking and talking, it's about how you talk and how you express yourself to your defenders and help them. Some goalkeepers just talk for the sake of it. You need to be clear in your messages. I was on fire and really fired up when I came into the team.'

Marcus Hall is under no illusion that both were quality goalkeepers, but for him Oggy's communication was hard to replace.

'The main difference was Oggy's voice,' he says. 'His constant shouting, and I don't mean that in a bad way. It was getting the defence into shape and giving commands out all the time. His bellowing voice behind me is what I needed as a young lad. He was the best pro I've come across in my career. You could hang your hat on Oggy, you knew what you were going to get. Magnus was a bit more dynamic but not as loud, maybe not as consistent as Oggy as well. I missed Oggy's voice behind the defence, but both were fantastic goalies.'

Oggy's legendary status is in no doubt, and Trond Soltvedt reveals that the veteran was held in the highest regard by everyone at the club from the top to the bottom. In fact, gaffer Gordon Strachan's reverence for his goalie could even turn an emphatic win into a right royal roasting.

'We always went to Scotland in pre-season, I think so we could win some games and get confident before the season started,' the Norwegian midfielder says. 'We were playing a pre-season friendly in Scotland and were winning about 7-0. It was a fantastic performance. The other team got a corner near the end of the game. Dion was always in the six-yard box for defending corners and he went to clear the ball with his head when Oggy screamed for the ball so Dublin let the ball go but a striker got in and scored. Dublin lost it a bit, which did not happen often, and he screamed at Oggy. When we got into the changing room Strachan was absolutely boiled red in his head and fucking hell, he threw around these tea cups. I had this nice sky-blue shirt on and my shirt got hit with one of those cups and he said, "Fucking hell, nobody is talking to

Oggy in that way again as long as I am the manager, he is the most professional player I ever played with." It was so quiet in the room. Strachan went out and smashed the door and went to the coach and sat in the front seat. This was after one of the best games we'd ever played, we'd won something like 7-1 but the manager went ballistic. I had to get a new shirt!'

Back to that opening day, and Hedman repaid the faith put in him by Strachan, but perhaps not in the way that you might expect. Rather than pulling off a string of saves, the Swede was instrumental in City's efforts going forward. His long kicks were often right where frontman Dublin wanted them.

'Magnus would always try and find me with his goal kicks,' says Dublin. 'What I told him to do was to put the ball towards the defender's head on my inside shoulder. If you kick the ball straight down someone's throat then the defender can see the ball is coming straight to him but he can't see me. If you kick it on to my head then the defender can see me and the ball. Magnus would kick the ball on to the defender's head so the defender had to keep an eye on the ball and wouldn't know where I was. I would come across from the outside to the inside and as soon as I did that Hucks would be making his run. At least half of the time I would win the header and Hucks would be on his way. That is something that we did all of the time. A nice low trajectory, not too high, I'd get across the defender, flick it on, Hucks is one-on-one, thank you very much, 1-0.'

That was the case on this particular August afternoon. Hedman's punt was guided on as Dublin beat Gus Poyet in the air. Huckerby charged through and looped the ball over Ed de Goey and into the net. Dublin evaded Poyet again to make it 2-0 with a fine header. Chelsea pulled one back but the Sky Blues got the win. It was a performance that showed that the Huckerby–Dublin partnership had every chance of beating their mammoth goal haul from the previous season.

'Dion and Huckerby bullied Chelsea,' Richard Shaw remembers. 'With Dion loving that physical challenge and Hucks running in and around him, we always fancied our chances. When you start the season like that it gives you real confidence that you can compete.'

It was a partnership that carried no secret plan. Defenders would have known what to expect, an aerial battle with Dublin, who was regularly a near-post target for set pieces, and the constant threat of Huckerby running over the top. Knowing what to expect was one thing, stopping it was another.

'We knew each other's game and were confident that we would score,' says Dublin of the strike partnership. 'Gary Mac must have got 15 assists one season when he would drop the ball into the near post and I'd head it in. I don't know how defenders didn't clock it, they just couldn't work out how I kept scoring at the near post. One time, Leicester had five defenders around me and I still scored. It was just what we did.'

Sadly, the optimism generated by the opening-day win quickly evaporated. The Sky Blues went on a poor run, failing to win any of their next seven league matches. Even worse, Dublin was nearing the exit door. Talk of his new contract had rumbled on for an age. A new deal had finally been signed but it included a clause that would see the striker alerted should an offer of a certain amount, believed to be £5.75m, come in.

'We couldn't get him to sign a new contract,' Bryan Richardson recalls. 'He'd just played for England at Wembley and won the golden boot, which was remarkable at a team that was not one of the heavy hitters. He didn't have a minimum release clause, he had a need to know clause. It said that if we had an offer in excess of a certain amount then we had to inform him. It was a silly clause really because if somebody is going to offer that then they've already tapped up the player or the agent. He signed the contract though, I think it was for £22,000 per week.'

Here's where it all gets a little murky. Blackburn came in with a bid for Dublin well above the amount stipulated in his contract. Richardson, perhaps sensing an opportunity to cash in on a 30-year-old player or maybe just passing on the details of the offer as stipulated in the new deal, informed Dublin. For Dion, the club's willingness for him to speak to Blackburn was an admission that they were happy to ship him out. The problem was, he had no intention of joining Blackburn. However, when a deal to stay in the Midlands and join Aston Villa came along it was a different story.

'Blackburn came in,' recalls Richardson. 'But, no doubt at all, Gregory was manager at Villa and Doug Ellis was chairman and they said to Dion he could go there and he wouldn't have to move house, and said, "Here's the deal for you." There's no question that the deal was already done.'

'The chairman said Blackburn wanted to sign me,' says Dublin. 'I told him I didn't want to go to Blackburn but he said they had offered £6.75m and I had to go and have a chat with them. When Villa found out they came in at £5.75m and I said to myself that if they wanted me to move to Blackburn then that meant they wanted me to move and they wanted the move. Because of that, I said I wanted to go speak to Villa. The chairman didn't want me to go to Villa, he wanted me to go to Blackburn because it was more money. When I found out that he was going to accept offers for me, then the floodgates were opened and other teams came in. Leeds came in as well. It was down to the chairman saying he wanted me to go to Blackburn. I didn't ask to leave. The rest is history.'

The history books show that Dublin was not involved in the next two matches before he sealed his move to Villa. Whether he refused to play remains a point of debate, but without their talisman the Sky Blues fell to a flat League Cup defeat against Luton. The second match was a league fixture with Arsenal, a game tragically remembered for the death of steward Ron Reeves afterwards. In the days that followed,

Dublin left in a move that cast a shadow over his legacy for many years to come.

'It turned very sour the way things finally panned out,' says Rob Gurney. 'I vividly remember Strachan hanging him out to dry by saying he had refused to play after the Luton game. It all came to a head there. You knew once Strachan had gone public with that there was no way back for him.'

'Leaving for Villa will always take a few points off,' Strachan says, assessing Dublin's legacy. 'But Dion did it for a long time for Coventry. He got in the England team. That was a great day for me because Kevin Keegan called me up and said he was going to call Dion up and he was going to play. I asked Kevin if I could tell Dion. I'd watched him work so hard, he did alright, went back to centre-half then when we put him back up front that was it, he was great. That was one of my best days in management to tell him that he was going to play for England.'

For some, it was the club that was in the wrong in the way the deal was handled.

'I don't know if Dion wanted to leave or if he was pushed out,' says Huckerby. 'I know for a fact that I was told that Coventry wanted him to leave. Players are on long contracts, if the club don't want to sell, then they don't have to. Dion was on a long contract, I was on a three-and-a-half-year contract. Any team in world football that loses their best players will struggle.'

'Dion spent five years at Coventry and he earned the right to speak to a big club,' adds Richard Shaw. 'I don't think the club treated him very well. He had given the club a lot and helped put them on the platform they were on. When he left it left a huge void. We didn't just lose a No.9, he was a captain, he was a leader of the group. That was a difficult time. It was a massive wrench to lose Dion.'

It was a huge blow for the club and, in particular, for Huckerby. The pair had looked as good as any front two in

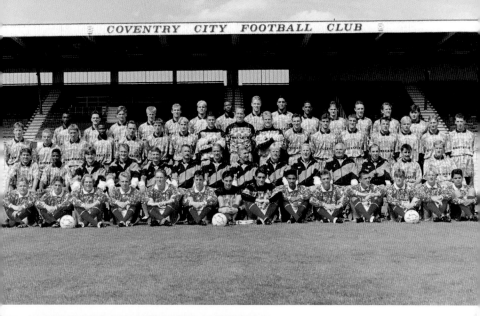

*Where it all began –
Coventry City's inaugural
Premier League squad in
August 1992.*

*Micky Quinn celebrates a
goal against Aston Villa on
Boxing Day 1992.*

Bobby Gould issues the instructions while Micky Quinn enjoys one of his opening-day treble at Highbury in 1993.

The much-missed Highfield Road, viewed from the sky in 1994.

Phil Neal joined Bobby Gould's coaching staff in 1992 but it wouldn't be long before he was in the managerial hot seat.

Ron Atkinson gets bums on seats for his Coventry debut against West Ham in February 1995.

Peter Ndlovu, John Salako and Dave Busst enjoy City's 5-0 win over Blackburn in December 1995.

Noel Whelan celebrates a sublime solo goal against Southampton on New Year's Day 1996.

Gordon Strachan dusts off his playing boots for an appearance in February 1996.

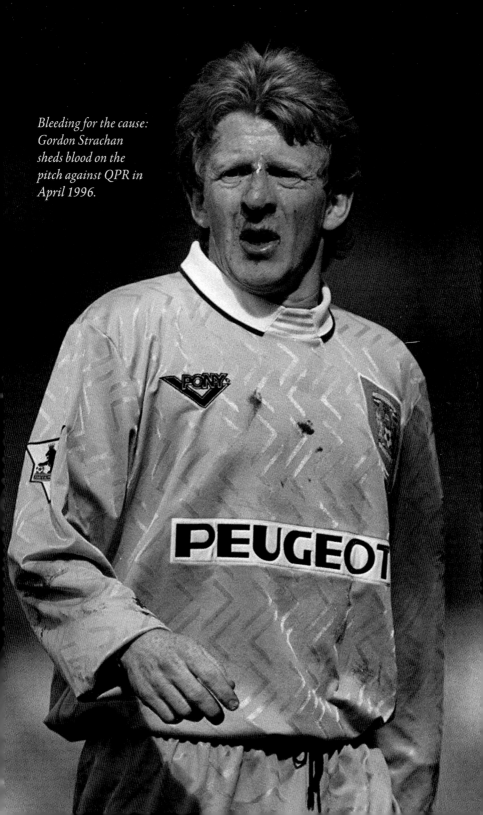

Bleeding for the cause: Gordon Strachan sheds blood on the pitch against QPR in April 1996.

Big Ron poses with then record signing Gary McAllister, a snip for £3m in 1996.

Darren Huckerby scores his first Coventry goal, against his former club Newcastle, in December 1996.

the country for the previous 12 months and now they had been ripped apart.

'Personally, I was devastated,' Huckerby says. 'We had just ripped it up the season before. Every defence feared us. We'd just beaten Chelsea at the start of that season with both of us scoring and then he was gone. All of the work we had put in over the last two seasons and it was just gone. Myself and Snowy [Noel Whelan] played up front after that and did quite well but I always thought as a front three with myself and Dion up front and Snowy on the left or right or just behind us was the perfect scenario. Losing Dion was a massive loss for the team and the dressing room. We lost one of our impact players, you knew he was going to score you 15–20 goals a season, but also when things are going wrong you look to players like Dion and Gary McAllister to get you through it.'

The man himself admits that had he stayed, there was the nucleus of a team that could have gone on to greater heights in the years to come.

'If that team had stayed together for another two or three seasons, that team would have easily been top half of the table if there had been a little bit of investment,' Dublin predicts. 'We could have just got better and better. I look back on that time fondly, I don't look back on it as a what if. I look back on it and think about what a great time that was. It was a brilliant five years that I had at Coventry.'

The brilliant five years came to an end and it wasn't just on the pitch that Dublin would be missed. I'm not exaggerating to say that every player I've interviewed for this book who was at the club at the same time as Dublin has mentioned in one way or another his huge influence off the field. Whether it be helping new players settle, organising team bonding or just setting the standards for others to follow, Dublin was a leader in every sense of the word.

'I was happy to have a leader role,' he says. 'When you go into a dressing room, it's quite daunting. Most of the time

I was a senior member of the squad and I just liked making people feel comfortable and part of the squad. I'd tell them good places to eat, where to park their car and everything like that. I just liked making people feel welcome and wanted them to know that if they had any problems they could come and see me and I'd try to put it right.'

'There was no one you'd rather go into battle with than Dion,' says Huckerby of Dublin's leadership role. 'He wasn't one who was always involved in the banter but he was a leader. When Dion said it was time to get to work or roll our sleeves up, we did. When he spoke, we all listened. You did what he said. We were lucky to have him. He gets a bad rep because he went to Villa. Let's be brutally honest, if he had gone to someone like Chelsea, the Coventry fans would just remember him for what a great player he was. If you look at his goals and what he did for the club, he was one of the best centre-forwards in the Premier League in an era when centre-forwards were unbelievable. The only downside is that he went to Villa. None of us really know the ins and outs of that move. We all find out later down the line that we have to go when the club decides to sell us.'

Dion wasn't the only striker who made a move away from the club in the early part of the season. Simon Haworth, having been signed from Cardiff the previous year for £500,000, was moved on to Wigan for a £250,000 profit. Haworth's career is best remembered for the high of his debut in a 4-1 League Cup thrashing of Everton, the aforementioned missed penalty against Sheffield United and, perhaps, a feeling of unfulfilled potential at Highfield Road. His move shows a different side to transfers in comparison with that of Dublin. Haworth's tale echoes those that I've heard from several players in the writing of this book. For Haworth, see also Laurent Delorge and Cobi Jones; young players moving to Coventry with minimal support. Haworth may have only been making the move from Wales but it's easy to forget that, at the time of his transfer to

Coventry, he was a teenager. Not just that, but a teenager who had problems just like the rest of us. These issues didn't just disappear because he was catapulted into a Premier League football club.

'Fans will probably see me as someone that they'd think came, flopped and went but I'd like to think it was more than that,' says Haworth. 'I was a young boy, my mum didn't drive, I was from a council estate in Cardiff, that was all I had known. I'd lost my dad, was thrown into the Midlands and told, "Here's a housing estate, buy a house on there and figure it out." I didn't drive. No one knew what I was doing at night after training. I wasn't doing anything wrong but I was sat about bored. Was I eating right? No one was there looking out for me. That has all been hugely improved since then. I lost my Premier League career because of that, I would say.'

Haworth was yet to set the world alight in a sky-blue shirt and, as he looks back today, there is a pang of regret that he didn't bide his time at Highfield Road.

'I was only 18 months into my contract,' he says. 'Leaving is a big regret. They told me they'd accepted offers from Brentford and Wigan and I was free to speak to them. That was telling me that I wasn't really wanted. I wish Strachan had said, "You're not going there, you're staying here." I had known Michael O'Neill from Coventry and he had gone to Wigan. I was a young boy without any advice or guidance. In hindsight, I should have stayed for longer and worked through it.'

Through the sales of Moldovan, Dublin and Haworth, the club had brought in more than £10m by early October. It was expected that a chunk of that cash would be spent on attacking reinforcements as three strikers had left since the summer with bit-part player Paul Hall the only addition up top. Somewhat surprisingly, only £650,000 was reinvested in attacking replacements, all of which was spent on John Aloisi.

The Australian had got off to a flying start in the second tier with Portsmouth.

'I think I had scored 17 goals in all competitions by November so I felt maybe a Premier League club might come in for me,' he recalls. 'Alan Ball called me into the office and told me that Gordon Strachan had been in contact and Coventry were interested. As soon as I spoke to Gordon Strachan it was a no-brainer. I had always wanted to play in the Premier League. Growing up in Australia I watched the First Division as it was then and it was something I badly wanted to be part of. When I spoke to Strachan, he told me all about the team and they had just lost Dion Dublin to Aston Villa. They had Huckerby and Whelan up front and he just wanted to get another striker.'

Steve Froggatt was another new signing. The winger had been brought in just weeks before the sale of Dublin. The latter's departure raised an eyebrow from the former Villa and Wolves man as he had been signed to supply crosses for Dublin. For Froggatt, he had the choice of Coventry or Bryan Robson's Middlesbrough. He went against his agent's advice and signed for Coventry.

'I went to see Bryan Robson and then came to see Gordon,' he says. 'It was a difficult choice. I'd always played in the Midlands and we had an 18-month-old and another one on the way, so it was a family decision. My agent wanted me to go to Middlesbrough because he felt they were a bigger club. I came to see Gordon, met the lads and got a really good feeling for it. It felt like a family club. It only took a day to make my mind up and say I wanted to join Coventry, which I don't think Gordon was expecting. I think he thought I was going to go to Middlesbrough!'

Froggatt was instantly taken by the team spirit he found in the Coventry dressing room.

'I used to come in early because I wanted a front-row seat in the dressing room because there was so much micky-taking and it was so funny,' he laughs. 'I didn't want to miss any of it! It's quite rare, but when I first came to the club there were no massive egos in the dressing room. The camaraderie was absolutely brilliant.'

'With Coventry, we needed that team spirit because we were up against it most weeks,' Marcus Hall adds. 'We were always fighting. We needed to be a close-knit group if we were going to survive in the Premier League. People like Dion and Darren Huckerby were the heartbeat of our team and once we lost that it became a lot more difficult. There was a group of Huckerby, Telfer and Whelan who were micky-takers. All of the time, literally. It was really harsh as well, and if you showed a bit of weakness then they'd go even more on you. You'd never get away with some of it now. It would go to places where you'd think if it went any further it would end up in a fight. You had the usual things of cutting up clothes and things like that and silly stuff but it always stayed on the right side of ever causing a fight and it was all in good spirits.'

Looking back, the remainder of this season feels very much like a transitional period. The club looked slightly rudderless having lost Dublin and it's testament to the players who remained that relegation never really seemed a genuine threat, despite losing our talisman so early in the campaign. Froggatt, Whelan and Huckerby were integral in stabilising the club during this time. All three stepped up and ensured that an attacking potency remained. The trio all found themselves on the scoresheet in a 3-0 win over Everton, live on Sky in November. Froggatt bagged the pick of the goals, a screamer from well outside the box that arrowed into the top corner.

'That game was particularly special,' he says. 'Any Sky game is a big game. I always liked the night atmosphere, it's always noisier at night. That performance laid the Dion Dublin ghost to rest. It showed that we could play well without Dion and win without him and gave us great confidence going forward for the rest of that season. I'm very fortunate that I've scored quite a few goals like that in my time. I hit two or three like that for Wolves. I giggle with that goal because I could just picture Snowy, Hucks and McAllister giving me pelters if it hadn't gone into the top corner, because I hadn't passed to them.'

The win was followed by a run of seven without a victory to see out 1998. The new year started with a bang though, as Huckerby notched back-to-back hat-tricks, one in the FA Cup against Macclesfield and then a week later in the league against Nottingham Forest. It was days like this that Huckerby was simply unstoppable.

'I had days like that where it didn't matter who I was playing against, it was physically impossible for them to stop me,' he says. 'Sometimes I was so quick and direct with my running that defenders couldn't do anything. All three were good goals against Forest but I think I could have scored a couple more in that game. Sometimes you know every time you get the ball you can make something happen.'

The rapid forward was adjusting well to life without his strike partner and was banging on the door for an England call-up.

'Two or three times in my career I probably should have got an England call-up,' he says. 'I know at that time England were blessed with some incredible forwards. It wasn't like it is now where it's Harry Kane and whoever else is around at the time. Then you were talking Ferdinand, Shearer, Fowler, Le Tissier, Sheringham, Owen just to name a few. I've always thought there were better players than me that haven't got caps but I think I'm better than some who did get caps. I'd have loved to have got a call-up for my mum and dad.'

Huckerby wasn't the only one stepping up to the challenge. Noel Whelan had endured some tough times since announcing his arrival at the club with a flurry of goals several years earlier. Undoubtedly a lively character, Whelan had run into some much-publicised problems, most notably putting his foot through a shop window in 1997, rupturing his Achilles tendon in the process and almost ending his career. This was the catalyst for Gordon Strachan and his wife Lesley moving Whelan into their family home for a stint to get him back on track.

'He lived with me for six weeks,' says Strachan. 'I'd known him since 16 and knew his dad and mum. I was like an uncle. I tried my best to look after him and so did Lesley. Lesley still thinks he's a smashing lad to this day [laughs]. I'm scared to tell Lesley the whole truth about Noel! We had to look after him because he was getting himself into some horrible situations, so I told him he was staying with us.'

'Gordon was the right person for me,' Whelan says. 'He knew I needed a family around me. He knew I was close to my family in Leeds and I guess I lost my way a little bit. I wasn't one to sit down and watch TV or play on a PlayStation. That wasn't me. I couldn't be around myself, I had to be out and about and around other people. I was hyperactive. My brain couldn't relax very much. I'm sure Gordon wishes I could have done and that would have given him less stress. He was fantastic with me. He brought me into his home when I needed him. He looked out for me. At the same time, I don't think he'd want to have changed me too much. People's personalities are important. I don't remember any of the times when I had done something wrong, getting dropped because of that. He knew that he needed me just like I needed him.'

For Strachan, Whelan's story is one that he speaks of clearly with sadness. The striker is discussed by fans and team-mates as one of the most talented players they've ever seen, someone who, as mentioned earlier in this book by the likes of Big Ron, should have gone right to the top.

'He could have had a great career,' Strachan says. 'It's a sad story but it's a warning to every footballer. You cannot play football like that. He did really well for Coventry for a year or so and then it went down when his lifestyle was poor.'

'He had everything apart from a stable home life,' adds David Burrows. 'If he had settled down and got married and had kids maybe he would have fulfilled his potential and played for England. Noel was a bit of a lad, he liked a good time. He hadn't settled down in his private life. Gordon really looked after him and put up with a little bit of stuff that he might not have put up with from other players because of his history with him. That's how Noel was, he played like that, he lived like that. As a player, he had everything.'

Coventry Telegraph chief football writer Andy Turner also laments Whelan not quite making the most of his undoubted talent, acknowledging that the striker was playing in a different era to today's sheltered and shielded stars.

'You have to remember at that time football wasn't as professional as it is now,' says Turner. 'Footballers aren't saints now but you don't have the drinking cultures, like the Manchester United drinking culture from the Bryan Robson days, with which Gordon Strachan I think struggled to fit in because he was one of the trailblazers in thinking about sports science and moving with the times. Young players earn lots of money and attract lots of attention. You get two types of lifestyles. There's the guys like Roland Nilsson, someone who used to weigh his food when he was injured to make sure that he didn't overeat and put on weight. That's how disciplined he was about his lifestyle and being at peak physical fitness. You've got that one extreme and at the other you've got young lads who want to go out and have a good time. Noel was a lovely character. You'd go down to Highfield Road and Noel would be sat there with Michelle the receptionist, who is unfortunately no longer with us, and Noel would just be sat behind reception welcoming guests and messing around. You don't really have characters like that these days.'

Whelan accepts that he did enjoy his share of nights out, but was always ready to deliver the following morning.

'When you're a footballer and you go out, you're a target,' he admits. 'The problem was people thought because I was a footballer I wouldn't react and that wasn't true. I'm a human being and if somebody threatens myself, a friend or a family member, and I classed my team-mates as family, then I would always stick up for them. I never changed, I always stuck to my values. I accept that I should have behaved better at times but sometimes the way you are takes over. There was a culture where you went out and drank. We would go out as a team, I would go out with Telf. But I knew that even if I came in at five in the morning I would still beat everybody at running in training. Nobody would touch me in running except maybe Telf, but we would have been out drinking together [laughs].'

By 1999, Whelan had got himself on track and was delivering on the pitch. He ended up hitting double figures and topped the goalscoring charts for the Sky Blues in 1998/99.

'You've got to believe in your own ability and, yes, Dion left but you've got to get on with it,' he says. 'I trusted my ability to score and create goals. I don't think we were any less strong [after Dion's sale]. You still had two players there with different attributes: Darren with his pace, who could do something out of nothing, and I always backed myself. We both stepped up and proved what a good striking partnership we were. We would both try things that other players wouldn't dream of trying, I think that's what made us a good partnership.'

By late February things weren't going quite so well for John Aloisi. The Australian forward had only managed one goal in a stop-start beginning to his Coventry career, but then came City's visit to Villa Park on 27 February. The Sky Blues went into the match in the bottom three, while Villa were up in fourth. Add in Coventry's wretched record at Villa Park and that the match would see Dublin line up in claret and blue and it was difficult to be optimistic.

'I remember sitting in the physio room beforehand getting some treatment and Steve Ogrizovic walked in,' says Aloisi. 'He knew I was starting the next day and he said, "You could go down in history here if you have a good game." He told me what a big game it was and that we hadn't had a good time at Villa Park, so this was a big opportunity and I should embrace it. I knew it was a big game but to hear it from someone like Oggy to not be nervous and to just embrace it was nice.'

Embrace it he most certainly did. Aloisi bagged a brace in a 4-1 win. Not even Dublin netting a penalty for Villa could spoil the day as a masterclass in the middle of the park from George Boateng powered the Sky Blues to victory.

'George Boateng really came to prominence that day,' says Froggatt. 'He stood out on the big stage and played ever so well that day. He was a real warrior on the park with a great engine getting from box to box. I made my Coventry debut against Villa earlier in the season and they beat us 2-1. We went and beat them 4-1 and I didn't get booed. I made a couple of goals. The next time I went to Villa Park with Coventry I got absolutely slaughtered. They'd obviously forgotten about me and then that 4-1 game reminded them of me!'

'That Villa win was a highlight of my time at Coventry,' adds Aloisi. 'I had a mixed time at Coventry because I was injured a lot, that was disappointing for me. That game was such a highlight. It was a great game. I scored at the end where the Coventry supporters were and they were ecstatic.'

Team	P	GD	Pts
16. Charlton	27	-6	27
17. Coventry	27	-10	27
18. Blackburn	27	-11	26
19. Southampton	26	-24	23

The victory lifted the Sky Blues out of the bottom three. They would not return to the relegation zone again all season. The win did have one unfortunate side effect though. It put Boateng very much on Villa's radar. Lest we forget, he had done all of the legwork with a silky run to make Viorel Moldovan's winner at Villa Park in the FA Cup the previous season as well.

'That performance got George the move to Villa,' Strachan says of the 4-1 win. 'We were at Everton later on that season and we were having a team talk and I looked up and George was sleeping. I crept up on him and the boys saw me and started shouting to George. I found out later on he was travelling to Amsterdam that week and the night before had spoken to John Gregory and Doug Ellis. I confronted him and it was hilarious. I said, "George, remember, I know you're a Christian and your mum's a Christian and you don't tell lies before you answer this: have you been speaking to Aston Villa behind our back?" And he said, "Yes!" His face was brilliant because he knew he couldn't tell a lie.'

Following the conclusion of the season, Boateng would indeed seal a £4.5m move to Villa, but before that we still had a few months to enjoy the Dutchman in a Coventry shirt. Meanwhile, Aloisi was looking to build on his brace as Charlton visited Highfield Road. The day didn't go quite to plan for him, as he ended up being sent off for slapping Danny Mills around the head.

'I felt good in that Charlton game but Danny Mills was just on top of me, stepping on my foot the whole game, just being a pain in the arse like Danny Mills is,' he recalls. 'I saw him not long ago in Australia when he was doing commentary and I told him then that he was a pain in the arse! I regret doing what I did in that game. It was a stupid thing to do and I lost my temper. I didn't even hit him that well. I was disappointed about that. If I'm going to get sent off I should have at least hit him properly. Thankfully, we ended up winning the game but it set me back because I was out for three games. I had been on a roll but then I didn't play for three weeks.'

Despite losing Aloisi, goals from Whelan and Soltvedt gave City a 2-1 win. Strachan was still far from happy, however.

'Gordon Strachan was not happy with me at all and that set me back a bit,' admits Aloisi. 'Strachan was a fiery character. His training sessions were really good, I enjoyed his training. He could lose it very quickly but I understand that now that I'm a coach. I can understand why he was getting frustrated at times. Probably as players we didn't see the reasons at the time but I understood why he got angry at me for getting sent off. I learnt a lot from him but I didn't want to get on his bad side, that's for sure, but sometimes I did.'

A typically inconsistent end to the season followed. Wins over Sheffield Wednesday and Southampton were followed by three defeats on the bounce against Everton, Middlesbrough and Leicester. The Middlesbrough match is best remembered for Magnus Hedman being clearly injured after a collision with a 'Boro player but still playing the full 90 minutes.

'I picked up a bad injury against Middlesbrough,' Hedman recalls. 'Strachan told me to stay on. I was in so much pain that I couldn't talk. I couldn't shout because of the pain. I said to Strachan that I had to come off and he gave me the hand to say, "No, you stay on, you stay on." It was the worst pain I have ever felt. I ended up paying for it, it fucked me up. I had to play with injections in the next games. That was by far the toughest game I ever had to play. I did everything I had to do for the team but it was very hard, I remember that pain like it was yesterday. I got that mentality from Strachan; you go in with your life and you do everything for the team. I tried to do that for Coventry every single time I was on the pitch. That game came from what Strachan put into my mind about not giving in no matter what.'

A win over Wimbledon before draws with Derby and Leeds saw out a campaign that, in all honesty, had fizzled out somewhat following the loss of Dublin. The Sky Blues finished a comfortable six points above the drop zone in 15th.

1998/99 league record with and without Dublin

	P	W	D	L	Pts
With Dublin	10	2	2	6	8
Without Dublin	28	9	7	12	34

Fans were looking for fresh blood to come in, a recognised striker to take Dublin's place and add to the options of Huckerby, Whelan and Aloisi. What most didn't expect was for Huckerby to be sold to Leeds in a £5.5m deal. It was news to Huckerby, too.

'I didn't want to go,' he says. 'It came out of the blue. I went into training and sat with Strach on the hill in between the two pitches at Ryton and told him that I didn't want to go. He said that Leeds was a big club and I told him I wasn't bothered about that because I wanted to stay at Coventry and play week in, week out. He told me that the club had decided that this was the way that they wanted to go. As soon as you hear that, you're done really.'

As the 1999/00 season neared, the club was still reeling from the loss of Dublin and had now sold Huckerby and Boateng. It looked like being a long, hard season ahead. Little did we know at the time, but the club was on the cusp of putting together one of the most exciting teams in its history.

10.

The Entertainers

IT IS astonishing to look back at Coventry squads from the Premier League era and note the amount of change that occurred in just a few short years. Examine the squad Phil Neal utilised, for instance, with the likes of Steve Morgan, Julian Darby, Ally Pickering and David Rennie and compare it to the one Gordon Strachan inherited when he took over. Many of those players had filtered down the leagues and been replaced by John Salako, Richard Shaw, Noel Whelan et al.

As the 1999/00 season neared, the Sky Blues were in the midst of a similar overhaul. This time, however, many of the departing faces were going on to what were perceived as bigger and better things. In quick succession, Coventry had lost Dion Dublin, Darren Huckerby and George Boateng. Looking at the squad list, there was a definite lack of attacking prowess going into the new campaign.

Thankfully, targets had been identified, including a pair of Moroccans – Youssef Chippo and Mustapha Hadji. The former arrived from Porto for £1.2m, while the latter joined in a £4m deal from Deportivo. Chippo reveals that the pair had first caught Strachan's eye a year earlier on the grandest stage.

'At the 1998 World Cup we were in a group with Brazil, Norway and Scotland,' he says. 'I think Strachan came and watched the Scotland games so saw me play there. He was impressed by the Morocco team in that last group game against Scotland and he started to follow my career from there. I was at Porto at the time and he sent scouts to watch me play for Porto. Then he came to watch me in a game for Morocco against Holland in a friendly. After that game he contacted Porto and the clubs agreed the deal.'

The move for 1998 African Player of the Year Hadji was a statement of intent both in and outside of the club.

'You forget how good Hadji was,' says Richard Shaw. 'We were in a training camp in Germany and Hadji walked through with about 25 agents. We were like, "Bloody hell, it's Hadij!" We were sat there eating our pasta and we just thought, "What?!"'

The Moroccans fitted the template for Gordon Strachan's Coventry – talented players with the right attitude and work ethic.

'They were really good boys, they blended into the dressing room straightaway,' says Steve Froggatt. 'I think Gordon must have had a certain MO that he wanted because you can't have too many big-time Charlies in the dressing room. That would disrupt a dressing room like we had. He always brought good men into the team.'

Not all the signings that summer were so successful, though. The club spent an eye-watering £2m on attacker Stefano Gioacchini, a player that I have precisely zero recollection of. A further £1m was spent on Runar Normann, while goalkeeper Raffaele Nuzzo arrived on a free.

The season began in distinctly underwhelming fashion. A pair of 1-0 defeats, against Southampton and Leicester, were followed by a 1-1 draw with Wimbledon. What looked like three winnable matches had yielded just one point. Then something incredible happened.

In the summer of 1999, Robbie Keane was one of the most sought-after young players in the country. Aston Villa looked at him long and hard, reportedly bidding £5.5m, but they would not go any higher. The Wolves striker had netted

16 league goals in the second tier the previous season and it was obvious that he was destined for the top. What wasn't quite so obvious was that his ascent would include a stop-off at Highfield Road.

Bryan Richardson and Gordon Strachan pulled the trigger while others dithered and a £6m deal was struck, making Keane the most expensive teenager in Britain. A bout of something rather nasty-sounding meant that Richardson took the lead on the transfer.

'Signing Robbie was absolutely huge,' Strachan admits. 'It was Bryan Richardson that did that one. I had a fever and was in bed for a couple of days. My wife told me we'd signed Robbie Keane while I was ill and I thought it was some kind of dream and I went back to sleep again! I recovered from this horrendous illness to discover we'd signed a genius.'

Strachan may have sat out the negotiations due to illness, but even so he remained a huge part of the teenager's decision to join the Sky Blues.

'There was interest from Aston Villa but they wouldn't pay the extra £500,000,' Keane says. 'Mark McGhee was at Wolves at the time and he was very close to Gordon Strachan. I got a phone call from Strachan. I met him and he's a character, I really liked what he had to say. It was a good club for me at that time with a good manager who had been a clever player so I knew he'd want to play a certain way. It was a good fit. Coming from the Championship, it was a good club for me to join, to play in the Premier League and the move suited both of us.'

It certainly didn't take Keane long to impress his new gaffer.

'His first training session, Gary McAllister had the ball and Robbie had one step towards it and then spins in behind and he's left the whole back four for dead,' Strachan recalls. 'He left Paul Williams on his backside and we all started laughing. We were wondering what we had here. I asked him who taught him that because it must have been a good coach to teach him to step up and then spin in behind and use the space in behind.

Robbie said, "Nobody. What do you mean? What did I do?" He'd probably seen someone do that once somewhere and locked it away in his brain.'

His team-mates were just as impressed as the gaffer right from Keane's first training session.

'I've never seen anything like him,' smiles Richard Shaw. 'He's the best young player I've ever seen. I stand by that to this day. I was gobsmacked. I'd seen him at Wolves. We paid £6m for him and us senior pros in the changing room were thinking, "Wow, I wonder how this is going to turn out." We knew he was a good player but we didn't know how good he was until he turned up. He turned up and I'm looking at him thinking, "Okay, let's see what you've got." Oh my god, we couldn't get anywhere near him in training. He didn't have Huckerby's pace but the timing of his movement was just ridiculous. He was playing two or three passes ahead of everybody else. What a humble guy as well, he wasn't a big-time Charlie at all. We played an eight v eight and Macca hammered me and said, "Is there any danger of you getting tight to [Keane]?" I just said, "Macca, he's all over the place!" [laughs].'

It wasn't long before fans got to see what all of the fuss was about. On Saturday, 21 August, Keane made his debut for Coventry at Highfield Road against Derby. Two minutes before half-time, he was twisting and turning near to the byline at the Derby end. He shot from a ridiculously acute angle and somehow the ball ended up in the net. I was sitting behind the goal at the opposite end and was sure it must have taken a deflection and would be an own goal. Nope. He had scored from an angle that most strikers wouldn't have even attempted a shot.

'I couldn't believe that goal,' says Shaw. 'I was on the halfway line, going, "Has that gone in?!" It was only when I saw the replay, I saw how clever he was. Talk about quick feet and decision-making – he had everything. It astounds me how good he was.'

Those who had followed Keane's early career closely wouldn't have been surprised by the unconventional way that he opened his Premier League account.

'If you look at my goals from Wolves, I liked clever and cheeky goals,' Keane says. 'I wasn't frightened to try things. I was confident and as a goalscorer you have to always make defenders think. I wasn't a typical number nine who would be a target man so I had to be intelligent in how I created space for myself. That first goal, coming into that team as a young lad for a lot of money, I wanted to hit the ground running and once I got that first goal I felt I belonged in the Premier League. Before that, people didn't know if I was just a young lad with some talent or whether I was going to actually make a name for myself.'

Keane doubled Coventry's lead and his tally for the day on 67 minutes. Froggatt, who had played with the Irishman at Wolves, threaded a through ball, which Keane latched on to, rounded Mart Poom and scored.

'I expected him to make that impact,' Froggatt says. 'When I was about 20 I watched Robbie make his debut for Wolves against Norwich and he scored a couple of goals that day at 16 years of age. Gordon asked me about Robbie and he told me what they were going to pay for him and I thought it was a lot of money for a young kid. I said, "Listen, he's a fantastic player but please don't lay this one on me!" He set the place alight.'

There was a sense of almost disbelief inside the stadium at what we were witnessing. Coming out of the ground a fan behind us said, 'I wonder how long we can keep him for.' We knew this wouldn't be a long-term relationship but it was one we were happy to enjoy the passions of while it lasted.

'In all the years I've been covering the club, Robbie Keane's debut is one of the best debuts I've ever seen,' Andy Turner raves. 'He ran the show from start to finish. He was this young kid and he was orchestrating things. It made you think, "My god, what have we got here?" He was that good.'

One thing that struck me, even as a teenager in the stands, was his confidence. He was just a teenager himself and yet he was demanding the ball from the likes of Gary McAllister, pointing exactly where he wanted it to be played.

'He had that confidence bordering on arrogance, all great strikers have that,' Froggatt adds. 'He wasn't a tall player, physically he wasn't that strong but what he had was incredible technical ability and a knowledge of where to run. He had an old head on young shoulders in terms of how he made his runs. The great players think a yard quicker than everybody else and Robbie did that and lost defenders because he was so intelligent on the pitch.'

Keane's signing, however, couldn't have happened without the sale of a cult hero – Trond Egil Soltvedt. The Norwegian was moved on to Southampton for the somewhat underwhelming fee of £300,000.

'Rosenborg rang me and asked if I wanted to come back,' Soltvedt says. 'They said they'd had a fax from Bryan Richardson saying if they could pay £300,000 they could sign me. They didn't have all of the money they needed to sign Robbie Keane from the Huckerby sale. This is what Strachan told me. I asked to speak to Strachan and I had asked Rosenborg to send me the fax and I showed this to Strachan. I felt like I was a player that Strachan really wanted at the club. He really looked after me so I was so surprised about this fax. I showed him and he banged his hand on the table and said he didn't know anything about it. He said it was up to me but it wasn't down to him. I wanted to believe that but in football you never know. I didn't want to go back to Rosenborg. Rosenborg had tried to give me a five-year contract to make me the best-paid player when Coventry signed me but I wanted to play in the Premier League because I loved English football. I'd been following English football since 1972, I supported

Stoke. We played West Brom afterwards in Cyrille Regis's testimonial and I came on and scored. I spoke to my friends Claus Lundekvam and Egil Østenstad and told them I could go for a very cheap fee and they told [Southampton manager] Dave Jones and he signed me. It's a shame because I really enjoyed my time in Coventry but that's life as a footballer.'

As one foreign import left, two more were enjoying their first days at the club. Chippo and Hadji settled quickly, the former impressing with his box-to-box engine and eye for a pass, while the latter showed a great footballing brain and quality on the ball. Chippo liked what he saw from his team-mates.

'I was very impressed, we had good players from all over the world,' he says. 'My first season was absolutely fantastic. The Premier League was a dream for me to play in. My dreams came true with the move to Coventry. The atmosphere at the games was great, the fans were absolutely fantastic.'

The Derby win was followed by four without a victory, including three defeats. It meant that, eight matches in, the Sky Blues had just five points and were only above the relegation zone on goal difference. They undoubtedly had talent going forward with Keane, Hadji, Chippo and McAllister. What they needed was someone to come into the midfield and hold things together, to allow the others to get forward. What they needed was Carlton Palmer. The leggy midfielder joined for £500,000 from Nottingham Forest. I must admit it wasn't a signing that filled me with excitement but I'm more than happy to file Carlton alongside Dennis Wise and John Hartson as players who I had no idea of how good they actually were before seeing them in the flesh in a sky-blue shirt. Palmer joined before a home match with West Ham in late September and he helped to transform the team. City ran out 1-0 winners that day thanks to a Hadji header, his first goal for the club. This kick-started a run of seven without defeat in the league. For Palmer, it was business as usual.

'I'm not blowing my own trumpet but I know what I do and I know what I bring to the team and I know what it does for the rest of the players in the team,' he says with trademark confidence. 'It's just about getting around people. It's not just about playing. It's about putting on people on a matchday. I'd put it on Chippo, I'd put it on Hadji, they knew that when I crossed the white line they knew what that was about, I was all about winning. You need to be a strong player to do that and if you do that then you need to perform because if you don't perform then the other players can point the finger at you and say, "You're telling us to do this, to track back, to pick up and you're not doing it." That put pressure on me and that was fine. They weren't in good form when I got there but what I do is I get around people. Where I go, we always win games, that's just the way it is. You've got to have somebody like me in your side. Look at all of the top sides, it's like Chelsea with Kanté, Man City with Fernandinho, West Ham with Declan Rice, you need those types of players to allow your flair players to play. Anybody who knows football knows that. Look at Pogba, he struggled at Manchester United. If I played alongside Pogba at Manchester United he would be the best player all day long. At Coventry it was set up for me to be the holding midfield player and to block off areas so that if Hadji went and left a hole or if Chippo went and left a hole then I would fill that hole. That was my job.'

The steel that Palmer added in the middle of the park certainly did the trick. Gary McAllister, in particular, benefited from Palmer's arrival, as he played with a freedom to get forward and pull the strings in midfield, safe in the knowledge that his fellow veteran was behind him, ready to pounce on any loose balls or do the defensive running. It was a partnership that quickly flourished in a way that it hadn't earlier that decade when the pair were together at Leeds.

'We didn't click at Leeds,' Palmer admits. 'I think that was about egos. We played well at Leeds but we didn't click like we did at Coventry. I think that was because we were both coming to the end of our careers, we had grown up and were matured. We were big players and big egos at Leeds; he was the captain and I was playing for England. We should have gelled because everything matches for us to complement each other, but we didn't. When I went to Coventry we became good friends and had a lot of mutual respect. One of the nicest things was when he got the move to Liverpool he said that I had played a large part in that. People forget that Macca could run. He wasn't just a ball player, he could run as well. The way we played was that Macca was able to get a bit further forward and find the space and then if that happened you were in big trouble because he could pick a pass and he could finish.'

Barry Quinn was a youngster just breaking into the matchday squad at this point on his way to making 11 league appearances in 1999/00. He certainly noticed the impact of Palmer.

'Carlton Palmer came in and made a big difference,' he says. 'As a footballer he wasn't the most easy on the eye but his presence and what he did for the team was amazing. The reason why Gary McAllister had his best season was probably because of Carlton Palmer, because Carlton was a presence, he just tidied everything up and allowed Gary Mac to go on and do his thing. Carlton would see the danger and cover the ground. He was about 34 then but still as fit as anything. He did the things that you wouldn't always notice and he was really good at protecting the back four. He allowed those top players, the Hadjis, Chippos, McAllisters, Keanes to go and do their thing.'

The attacking talent was certainly doing its thing, as seen in the goals that were flowing in. October saw draws with Everton and Sheffield Wednesday fall alongside a 4-1 win over Newcastle and a 4-0 hammering of Watford. The Newcastle victory is best remembered for Paul Williams thwacking a 30-plus-yard shot past Shay Given for without doubt the finest goal of his career. It was hit from so far out that, as the defender swung his boot at the ball, someone behind me in the stand shouted, 'Clear it!' To be fair, it was at the opposite end to where we were sitting, so perhaps it looked further out from our vantage point!

By the time Aston Villa rolled into Coventry for a *Monday Night Football* match in November, the Sky Blues had a new striker on their books. Cédric Roussel had been spotted by European scout Ray Clarke and a deal was made, at first on loan, to allow Gordon Strachan to run the rule over the strapping Belgian target man.

'I first saw him playing against Scotland under-21s because Gordon's son was playing for Scotland,' Clarke recalls. 'Cédric played and he was a big lad, maybe not the quickest but he held the ball up. Players like him are now at a premium. Cédric gave you options, especially with Robbie Keane. Gary McAllister said to me that he loved Cédric. He said he'd get on the ball and he could go bang, straight into Cédric and he'd hold the ball up and you'd have Robbie Keane doing his runs off him.'

Roussel had impressed as a young forward at Gent, where he was enjoying a successful second season. Nevertheless, it came as a shock when he got the call to say that the Sky Blues were interested.

'My agent came to me and asked if I would be okay with the possibility of playing in England,' he says. 'I said, "Are you crazy? That is my dream!" Gent were okay for me to go on loan first. Coventry needed strikers; John Aloisi and Noel Whelan were injured and only Robbie Keane was fit. My agent said I would play some fantastic games in the three months, games against Chelsea, Arsenal, a derby against Villa, Newcastle ... I said, "Wow, okay, let's go!"'

It was a huge upheaval for Roussel, a 21-year-old tasked with settling in a new country and adjusting to a completely different level of football.

'It was my first time leaving home,' he says. 'My agent said he would come with me for a few weeks. My dad said not to worry because he would come to see me and spend time with me. I was sure, though, that it was the place for me because I was big and strong. The only thing was the rhythm of the game because in Belgium it is a lot slower. The training is harder and longer as well. In the first couple of weeks I was going back to my flat and sleeping all day because I was so tired. It was three hours' training in the morning and then I'd often stay with Gordon Strachan and a keeper for finishing in the afternoon. I was happy to do that, it was no problem. I'd get home at 4pm or 5pm and just sleep. But after the first training session I thought I could do well at Coventry. In my head I wasn't there just for three months. I was looking further, I was going to earn a contract and stay for many years. I settled well, Leamington is a very nice town. I was helped by Laurent Delorge. It would have been hard to go back to reality in Belgium after three months.'

Delorge was a fellow Belgian who also made the move to Coventry in 1999. Another Ray Clarke-approved signing, there were high hopes within the club for the skilful winger, who had signed a five-and-a-half-year contract upon moving from Gent in 1999. Things didn't go so well for Delorge, however, after he suffered a broken leg on his debut for the reserves shortly after joining.

'I remember going into the tackle in the middle of the pitch,' he recalls. 'I changed my mind midway into the sliding tackle as I thought I could get the ball otherwise. My left leg just got stuck and I twisted around it without any contact from another player. I ended up with a spiral break of the fibula bone of my left leg. I heard and felt it break so I knew straightaway that it was broken. Mr Strachan and his family took me in for the night since I had just arrived in the UK and nobody was with me.'

Delorge's Coventry career never recovered, hampered further by a torn hamstring shortly after his recovery from the broken leg. Eventually he would be sold to Belgian side Lierse SK in 2002, before spells at a handful of clubs, including Anderlecht and Ajax.

Back to Roussel, he was immediately struck by the quality that surrounded him at Ryton.

'When I signed for Coventry,' he says, 'I saw the quality on the training ground straightaway and I said, "Oh my god." I had a very good friendship with Youssef Chippo and Mustapha Hadji. We were a team of friends. We could beat anybody. We were giving any team a game, Chelsea, Man United, Arsenal – no problem. They knew that playing Coventry would be a difficult game. In a team you need two or three special players and we had Gary McAllister, a fantastic captain, and Robbie Keane who was different class. Behind them we had players like [Paul] Williams and Carlton Palmer who were great also. They knew how to play with me and knew my qualities. They knew the kind of passes I needed, they didn't give me the ball over the top because they knew I couldn't run so fast, but if I had my back to the goal I could get a touch or give a good pass. I was a player to aim for with a ball to get the team up the pitch.'

Roussel quickly began to make an impact. Just eight minutes into the match with Villa he met a fired cross from Robbie Keane with a bullet near-post header to put City in front. The Sky Blues fans were in raptures, taking great pleasure in taunting Villa boss John Gregory. The crowd reaction would have been no surprise to Roussel, as he had been briefed on the importance of the game before kick-off.

'We went to the hotel on Monday morning and Hadji came to me and said, "You know that this game is very, very important for the fans. They hate each other, they want to kill each other and we have to win this game,"' he says. 'I didn't remember from Belgium hearing that Coventry against Villa was a big game but Hadji said, "It's bigger than the games against Arsenal and Chelsea. You will see tonight, it will be very tense, very passionate." I said, "Woah, okay, okay." I got my first goal and got the assist for Robbie. It was the best way to introduce myself to the fans. I remember when the ball hit the net, oh my goodness, the noise of the fans was so amazing. It was so loud. From that moment I knew I didn't want to go back to Belgium, I wanted to play games like that every week.'

It wasn't all Coventry, though. Dion Dublin (who else?) levelled the scores just before half-time but it was to be Robbie Keane's day – the man that Gregory had refused to shell out an extra £500,000 for in the summer. A Chippo cross was flicked into the net by Keane for what would prove to be the winner.

'A lot of the build-up to that game was about Villa not paying the extra £500,000 for me,' Keane recalls. 'So, to score the winner in that one, the little side-foot past David James, it had a little extra spice because of all of the talk beforehand.'

It was on this night that I first realised the quality of this team. This was an attacking force that played with an excitement to rival even the best of the Dublin–Huckerby– Whelan days. The abundance of star power wasn't lost on the manager, either.

'Robbie sent me a video the other day of him scoring a ridiculous goal against Aston Villa,' says Strachan. 'I watched the highlights and was thinking, "That's a good player, there's another good player, that's another good player there!" Wonderful.'

Team	P	GD	Pts
9. Chelsea	13	+8	21
10. West Ham	14	+2	21
11. Coventry	15	+6	20
12. Everton	15	+2	20

If the Villa win was wonderful then what was to come was nothing short of spectacular. After a disappointing pre-Christmas spell that included defeats to Leicester and Liverpool and a draw with Southampton, the Sky Blues found themselves 13th in the table when they welcomed fourth-placed Arsenal to Highfield Road on Boxing Day, again in front of the Sky cameras. The match would go down as one of the most entertaining performances in the club's Premier League history.

Roussel hadn't quite hit the heights since that Villa performance and was expecting to, at best, start on the bench. He was more surprised than anyone to hear that he was in the first XI.

'It was Christmas and my family and best friends were in England,' he says. 'I didn't know I was playing when I got to the stadium. I was in the toilets and Gordon came in and asked if I was ready for the day. I said yes, I thought I would be watching the game from the stands with my friends. He said, "I think you are the best solution to giving their big guys trouble at the back." I said, "Woah, I'm starting?" He said not to worry and that I should just run over them, fight, win the duels, be stronger and then Robbie next to me would make the difference. I went out for the warm-up and saw my friends as I was going out. They were surprised I was going out for the warm-up and they asked if I was on the bench. I said I was starting and I could see on their faces that they were scared for me, and they said, "Oh my god, you're going to start against this team of Henry, Bergkamp and Suker? Enjoy it!"'

He most definitely enjoyed it. Roussel gave Arsenal's iconic back five an absolute battering, getting two assists in a 3-2 win.

'I was named man of the match,' he says. 'My friends were waiting outside the stadium for an hour because I had to do interviews and get the trophy. My brother said I had taken my time and I explained it was because I was man of the match and I showed him the trophy and then he started crying and said he was so proud of me.'

Carlton Palmer once again anchored the midfield and on the night Arsenal could not keep a handle on Coventry's attacking talent, with McAllister, Hadji and Keane all getting on the scoresheet, the latter with a gravity-defying flicked finish that somehow found its way past David Seaman.

'If you looked at the Arsenal team, it was *the* Arsenal back four,' Keane says. 'In the tunnel you looked at how big they were compared to me, they felt huge. They were a top team as well but that season with the crowd behind us and the way that we played, we always gave teams a game. My goal is one that stands out, the little flicked chip past David Seaman. That's up there with one of my favourite goals. I knew keepers always take a step to the right when the ball comes over to that side. That's something I had studied as a player, I used to watch keepers and how they moved. I thought if I could just get a little something on it I had a chance because of the way Seaman had shifted to the other side. It was instinct. They're the finishes that I liked, the clever finishes that take the keeper off guard, you've got a better chance to score if you do that. I had some natural talent and was confident in front of goal. Those kinds of finishes are the kinds that you can't really work on. They happen fairly quickly and you need to have that quick thought process to be able to score, you might only have half a second. I put in a lot of hard work to get to that point but it's hard to work on things like that.'

'We were a decent team with Robbie Keane and company,' Palmer assesses. 'We took Arsenal apart, with your Petits and Henrys. We played a brand of football that was open and attacking. We got out at teams. I really enjoyed being at Coventry. 3-2 flattered Arsenal. They said afterwards that we were hanging on. We weren't hanging on, we defended very, very well and that's just part and parcel of the game. If you can see a game out then that's part and parcel of football. If you look at the chances that we created in that game, we should have been out of sight. We were a good side. A good football team has to have characters and personality and that team had characters and personality.'

It was another match where the Roussel–Keane partnership really shone.

'Robbie was such a talented player and we worked together in training,' says Roussel. 'The manager made sure we played together in all of the small games in training and we worked on this partnership. Gordon knows football better than me, and he said, "You two are going to be a big deal in the Premier League." He was the guy to play with me, he was the perfect player for me. He had amazing movement. When I went for a header he knew where the ball was going to go. It was such a great opportunity to play with him. He was happy to give me the ball and I was happy to assist him for goals. We scored goals but also gave a lot of assists between each other. The flick-on for the second goal, there was still a lot for Robbie to do, I just wanted to give him a good pass. He knew what to do because he was such an intelligent player and so talented. We worked a lot on our partnership on the training ground.'

'I'd played with people like Don Goodman at Wolves, someone who was good in the air and Cédric was another who suited me,' Keane adds. 'He was a big guy who was good in the air and I was good at reading flick-ons. I liked to play in what you might call the nine-and-a-half role where you would drop off and come and get the ball whereas Cédric liked to stay up. We hit it off quickly and got an understanding of where each other would be. That was a really good partnership. He was a good player and we suited each other well with me dropping off and him as the target man.'

Following the match, Roussel was given a huge seal of approval from none other than Arsène Wenger.

'I used to be quite friendly with the Arsenal chief scout Steve Rowley,' Ray Clarke says. 'He came on the phone to me after we beat Arsenal 3-2 and said, "I've had my boss on the phone talking about your striker, where'd you get him from?" I told him and he said he had just battered Adams and Keown. He also rang me about Laurent Delorge, asking where we got him from, and he said three of Arsenal's scouts had been ringing him saying they had to look at him.'

The next league fixture saw an extraordinary match with Chelsea in which Coventry twice led but were twice pegged back almost straight from the kick-off in a 2-2 draw. Roussel scored one of the goals that night and he netted twice in a 3-2 defeat at Old Trafford before scoring in a 3-2 win over Sunderland at Highfield Road. The latter brought perhaps the greatest 20-minute spell I've ever seen from a Coventry team. City absolutely blew Sunderland away and were three goals ahead within 17 minutes, thanks to efforts from Keane, Hadji and Roussel. Unfortunately, that wouldn't be the lasting memory of the match. That's instead a shocking challenge by Nicky Summerbee on Steve Froggatt. The tackle, which forced Froggatt off after just ten minutes, didn't even yield a yellow card, but would have long-lasting repercussions for the Coventry winger, who by now had shuffled back into defence.

'I went to Gordon and told him that I wanted to play left-back,' Froggatt says. 'When you play left-wing in a team that is in the lower half of the table you can feel like you're not getting into the game as much as you want to as a wide man. I had played left-back and left-wing back at my other clubs and I said to Gordon I wasn't enjoying playing left-wing and I wanted a chance at left-back. He did that and I was playing well because I always did well running on to the ball. The day I lost my career I was at left-back against Sunderland. I thought I would see out my career at left-back for Coventry but obviously it didn't happen that way.'

It was a crying shame, particularly as Froggatt had earlier in the season earned a call-up to Kevin Keegan's England squad. The call-up came after Froggatt's impressive display in the 4-0 win over Watford – yet another cracking performance that season in front of the Sky cameras.

'I tended to play well for whatever reason in the Sky games,' Froggatt says. 'My call-up was on the back of that Watford game. I was lucky in that I was rare as I was left-footed. In the England squad at that time Jamie Redknapp was playing left-midfield. I played with Jamie in the under-21s, he's not a left-sided player, he's a central midfielder. It was a square peg in a round hole and Keegan needed a left-footer as an outlet, so the stars aligned a little bit. I remember the first game I played for Coventry after my call-up, it was against Bradford. I went up there and got pulled into the Bradford dressing room and there was Lee Sharpe and Dean Saunders. They gave me a big hug and congratulated me. I will never forget the reaction from the Coventry fans when I ran on to the pitch that day. It was the most incredible day and I was so proud to have a sky-blue shirt on. I knew what it meant to Coventry fans. At Villa they were full of internationals, Wolves had Steve Bull but at Coventry they only had Dion in the last 20 or 30 years who had played for England. The pride I had not just for myself but for my football club was incredible. I think it's a great shame for myself and for the Coventry fans that I never got the cap that would have come.'

Froggatt admits that he loved the dressing room banter at Coventry, but he thought he was the victim of a practical joke when Gordon Strachan informed him of his England call-up.

'At first, I thought it was a wind-up,' he admits. 'When Gordon called me into the office I was waiting for Willo and Shawsy to jump out laughing. These wind-ups happened all the time. I was sat in front of the gaffer and he must have wondered why I was sat there smiling. I was just waiting for

Willo and Shawsy! Strachan said, "This is not a joke, by the way." He pulled the letter out and I realised then that it was real. Gareth Southgate picked me up from my house and looked after me for the whole ten days, he was fantastic. It's quite a scary thing going into your first England squad. It's really nerve-wracking because you don't feel like you belong and you're playing with the likes of Beckham and Scholes. You think, "Woah, this is a different level now."'

Froggatt didn't make it off the bench for England's Euro 2000 play-off tie with Scotland but was assured by Keegan that he would make his debut in forthcoming friendlies against Ukraine and Brazil at Wembley. But, before those matches came around, the Summerbee tackle put Froggatt out of action. Determined not to miss out on his chance for his country, he tried to make a quick return just a month later in a 1-0 defeat away to Aston Villa.

'I made a comeback at Villa Park when I shouldn't have,' he admits. 'My ankle wasn't right. I had a couple of big challenges and that finished it off. I think my ankle was hanging by a thread, basically, from the Summerbee tackle, and then the other tackles finished it off.'

Froggatt would miss the next two league fixtures before attempting another comeback and playing four more matches, but he never recovered and was then sidelined for the rest of the season and the entire following campaign before calling time on his career. He played his final professional match shortly after his 27th birthday. He recalls that the career-ending tackle hadn't been his first run-in with Summerbee.

'We'd always had a bit of bad blood,' he says of the Sunderland winger. 'I'd played against him a few times and he was quite mouthy. I used to love the banter so I'd chirp back at him. We played at the Stadium of Light a few months earlier and how I didn't break my leg on at least four occasions, I don't know. At half-time Gordon said I had to look after myself because they were trying to break me in half.

Record breaker! Oggy receives an award from George Curtis before breaking the Sky Blues appearance record against Middlesbrough on 28 December 1996.

The familiar sight of Dion Dublin and Darren Huckerby saluting a goal (while Paul Williams gets in on the act!)

Dion Dublin and Noel Whelan celebrate a famous win at Anfield in 1997.

Mark Hughes and Gianfranco Zola curse their mismatched kit as they fall to defeat against the Sky Blues in April 1997.

Steve Ogrizovic and Paul Williams celebrate the 1997 'great escape' at White Hart Lane.

Dion gets the international call-up his Coventry form deserved in February 1998.

All smiles, for now. Steve Ogrizovic and Alan Kelly shake hands ahead of the FA Cup quarter-final penalty shoot-out in 1998.

George Boateng salutes the visiting fans after City's 4-1 win at Villa Park in February 1999.

Robbie Keane scores the deftest of goals against Arsenal on Boxing Day 1999.

Mustapha Hadji brought plenty of flair to the club following his move from Deportivo.

Gordon Strachan in the heat of battle on the touchline in January 2000.

John Hartson ruffled some feathers following his move from Wimbledon but arrived too late to save City.

A defiant fan insists we'll be back, upon relegation at Villa Park in 2001. It hasn't been a smooth journey since.

There was obviously something going on down at Highfield Road. Afterwards there was absolutely no apology. Nothing. I saw him a few years later at the Etihad. He was there with his dad and when he saw me he went white because he thought I was going to kill him. Do you know what I did? I went up and said, "No hard feelings." I didn't want to go through my life being bitter and twisted because unfortunately it's an occupational hazard of being a footballer. I was really lucky to have eight to ten years in top-flight football. I thought I would be the bigger person and get it over and done with. He did say to me that wherever he goes he gets absolutely slaughtered by Coventry fans! I told him there wasn't a lot I could do about that! I look back with sadness now that the fans didn't get the chance to see me play for Coventry for another three, four, five years. To this day that fills me with enormous sadness because it feels like I have unfinished business.'

As the season entered its final third, inconsistency, that familiar foe, reared its head once more. A potential turning point in the campaign came a few months earlier, at the tail-end of January in the FA Cup. Comfortable wins over Norwich and Burnley had set up a fifth-round tie at home to Charlton. The Sky Blues were without Hadji and Chippo, who were away on international duty, but looked to be cruising to victory thanks to a Roussel brace in the first 21 minutes. But Charlton came back to level the scores before half-time. Even all these years later I can still hear the voice of the supporter in front of me in the stands that day saying, 'They've nicked it,' as Andy Hunt scored Charlton's winner with just two minutes left. It felt like a cruel defeat, particularly for the Moroccans, who could have returned for a quarter-final tie. Even more galling, the last eight of the competition was free of Manchester United, Arsenal and Liverpool and included the likes of Gillingham, Tranmere and Charlton's eventual opponents, Bolton.

'I was very sad to lose against Charlton because we had a chance to get to Wembley,' says Roussel. 'Some big teams were already out and we had a chance against a Championship team. I scored two goals in the first 20 minutes and was thinking it would be four or five. For that first 20 minutes there was only one team on the pitch. After that they came back and won 3-2. It was unbelievable. In the dressing room everybody was kicking themselves. We knew we had lost the chance to go to Wembley.'

'That was disappointing,' says Palmer. 'The game was won. We threw the game away. It was bad defending. When you get results like that, sometimes it defines your season. It was disappointing but that's football. Sometimes it defines yourself or sometimes it galvanises you. In our case it had a disruptive effect on us.'

That disruptive effect saw a dip in form from February onwards. Following the aforementioned 3-2 win over Sunderland, there were four losses in a row. A narrow win over Everton, thanks to a goal from the superb McAllister, and a 4-0 smashing of Bradford came next but then came six defeats in the final eight matches of the season, including a 5-0 hammering against West Ham. Relegation never looked a threat throughout the season, but at the same time a squad with this much talent would have perhaps expected to have pushed into the top half. The Sky Blues instead remained just outside the top ten before slipping down to 14th by the end of the season. Many of the poor results that season were away from home. Gordon Strachan's men won an impressive 12 out of 19 home matches but famously didn't win at all on the road, picking up just seven points away from Highfield Road. It was an anomaly that left fans and players alike dumbfounded.

'As a player you don't know the reason [for the poor away form],' says Roussel. 'We were wondering how it could happen because we could beat anybody at home. We were trying to play the same football away from home. We were an attacking team but sometimes away from home you need to be a little bit more careful. We wanted to play attacking football and create chances and maybe that wasn't always realistic. Sometimes away from home we might be 1-0 up and try to score a second or a third when sometimes you are better to be more careful and protect 1-0.'

'If people had an answer then it wouldn't happen,' Marcus Hall adds. 'You don't go into an away game with a different mindset. We never went out to be defensive, we tried to play to the strengths that we had. Sometimes you just get stuck in a rut and no matter what you try you can't get out of it. There's no way we should have gone through the season without winning away from home. It's ridiculous. You can question the mentality but I know as a player that you go into it with the same mentality as the home games. Every game we were thinking, "Oh, we'll win this week," but it just went on and on. It was a freak season.'

1999/00 Home and away record

	P	W	D	L	Pts
Home	19	12	1	6	37
Away	19	0	7	12	7

Within this period, Roussel made his move to the club permanent in a £1.2m deal, despite reported interest elsewhere from the likes of Spurs. There's little doubt that the striker could have pulled in a fatter contract elsewhere, but there was only one team he wanted to sign for.

'When I was on loan and I signed my contract Gordon said they wanted me to sign a five-year contract but it was impossible because Coventry couldn't compete with wages at teams like Tottenham, Arsenal and Newcastle,' Roussel says. 'My answer was, "You have given me the chance to realise my dream to play in the Premier League. I am settled here.

I love Leamington. I love the stadium, I love the fans and I am starting games. I don't even want to see the salaries of Tottenham and the others, I just want to sign. I don't even want to know [the wages], I just want to stay at Coventry." Gordon said he had never heard that before and he was ready to cry because I was a gentleman. I wasn't a gentleman, I just recognised that he had given me so much. I just wanted to sign the contract and I wanted that from the first day I arrived at Coventry.'

As one new face sealed his permanent arrival, a club legend prepared to depart. As the season drew to a close, the curtain came down on the career of an absolute giant of Coventry City. Steve Ogrizovic, with 600 career Coventry appearances to his name, made the decision to hang up his gloves after 16 years at Highfield Road to take up a coaching role at the club.

'I could have potentially stayed as a player but I think that would have not been the right decision because Magnus was number one, Chris Kirkland was coming through and I was in the way really,' he says with typical modesty. 'I thought about going down the leagues and carrying on playing but then I thought, "God, I'm 43! I'm pushing my luck a little bit." My body was starting to tell me it was time. The years were catching up with me. Gordon asked me if I wanted to go into coaching with the academy. I was really indebted to him for that opportunity and I felt doing that was the right thing for me.'

There was time to notch up appearance 601 before the end of the campaign as Oggy was recalled to the starting line-up for the final home match of the season, against Sheffield Wednesday.

'I didn't expect to play in the last home game of the season but Gordon said he was going to put me in because I'd been at the club for all of these years and he wanted me to play in that final game,' he says. 'That was a lovely touch from him.

The reaction I got from the players, the fans, from everybody was something I will always cherish.'

I recall watching on that day from the stands as City brushed Wednesday aside, leading 4-0 as we entered the final ten minutes. On 81 minutes, Gilles De Bilde pulled back a consolation goal for the visitors. I still remember seeing Oggy's reaction to the goal. He beat the floor with his fist, clearly angered by the goal. Here he was, ten minutes from the end of his career in a match that in the grand scheme of things didn't mean a whole lot, one that we were 4-0 ahead in, and he was livid to have conceded a goal. For me, that showed the standards that he expected of himself, and his team, right to the end.

'The icing on the cake would have been a clean sheet,' he admits. 'It was a great occasion. I felt a little bit self-conscious doing a lap of honour but everyone insisted that I did one. The fans were absolutely brilliant. Moments like that are why you get into professional sport, it's for memories like that that you can cherish forever.'

The match was also marked by a brace for McAllister, taking his tally for the season to 13 goals across all competitions in 42 appearances. For context, he had managed 12 goals in his previous 85 matches for the club. It was an astonishing season for McAllister, not just for his goalscoring but also for his creativity in carving out chances for Hadji, Roussel and Keane. The midfielder's contract was up at the end of the season and there was speculation about whether he would sign a new deal or leave on a free. In the dressing room after the Sheffield Wednesday win, the thoughts of one of his team-mates turned to what the skipper's decision would be.

'We were playing against Sheffield Wednesday and Macca's contract was up,' recalls Richard Shaw. 'We were in the changing room and I was looking at Macca and I asked him what he was doing at the end of the season. He said he was keeping his options open. In my head I was thinking he was getting older and he might drop down to the Championship.'

Shortly after the end of the season McAllister didn't drop down to the Championship – instead he signed with one of the giants of English football.

'He rolled up at Liverpool and had another two years and won five trophies,' laughs Shaw. 'That wasn't a bad move. We really missed him the next season.'

Ah, the next season. Before that, Coventry rounded off 1999/00 with a 1-0 loss at already-relegated Watford – proof if it were needed that they could have played every team again and still not picked up an away win that season. While there was some embarrassment in the club's failure to win away, the season had provided so many highlights at Highfield Road. The wins over Arsenal and Villa, of course, stick out, but once Keane had arrived every home game was a joy. The Moroccans provided so much flair and excitement too and McAllister and Palmer were both fantastic. But, if fans had been spoiled with some of the home performances in 1999/00, then they were about to come back down to earth as the club's 34-year stay in the top flight came to an end.

11.

The End

ALL GOOD things must come to an end. The 2000/01 season is permanently etched in the minds of Coventry fans for all the wrong reasons. It was a painful, bruising campaign that ended with the club's departure from the Premier League after 34 years at the top table of English football. It transpires today, however, that Gordon Strachan sensed something was wrong that campaign and attempted to step aside in early September 2000.

'After the fourth game that season I said to Bryan [Richardson] that I thought I'd done enough,' he admits. 'I said I'd given my all, I'd played reserve games, player-coach, player-manager – I was shattered and said I thought he needed to get someone else in to kick on again. Bryan and my wife convinced me to stay. I knew myself I was running on empty. I didn't know if I could keep reinventing the team. I just felt it was one season too long. But people convinced me that it would be alright. I think with that and the recruitment not being right, it was a problem.'

Recruitment was a huge issue that season thanks to the one-two body blow and knockout punch of Gary McAllister and Robbie Keane leaving the club. McAllister had moved to Liverpool on a free, while Keane's single season in the Premier League had put him on the radar of every top club on the Continent. In the end it was Inter Milan who landed the Irishman. The Italian giants came in with a £9m bid. City countered with £15m before a £13m compromise was reached.

It meant another rebuilding task for Strachan, something that he sees as being par for the course at a club like Coventry.

'When you get Robbie Keane, your job is to make him better,' Strachan says. 'I told him I didn't mind if he went to Man United, Barcelona, whoever in a couple of years because if he did that then he'd done well and made us successful. Anyway, he lasted 11 months. I asked if I could have a word with him and I told him, "Inter Milan want to buy you, they're going to offer you X amount each week and you're going to play up front with Ronaldo – have a think about it and get back to me [laughs]." Every time I see him I say, "Robbie, you never got back to me!" 'I was happy to see these guys go on and do well.'

'Gordon called me into the office and said they'd had a bid from Inter Milan,' Keane recalls. 'He said, "I don't want you to go, but you have to go, you can't turn this down." He told me it was an opportunity that he didn't know how I would be able to turn it down. I wasn't looking to leave but the bid came in. It was a shame I was only at Coventry for a year. The club was brilliant to me and the fans were amazing. I hope I gave enough to the fans in that year to show how much I enjoyed the club and the fans. Unfortunately, I haven't been back there to watch a game since leaving. I'd love to go back one day and thank the fans.'

With that, the club lost Keane, one of the most talented players to ever wear the Coventry shirt, and McAllister, the talismanic captain. The pair's importance can be seen in their tally of 23 of the 47 league goals scored the previous season. It wasn't just the impact on the pitch, though; McAllister was a huge figure on and off the field and wasn't going to be easy to replace.

'To lose Gary McAllister, that was a massive loss,' says John Aloisi. 'He would know when the team needed picking up. He would know when the team needed to remain calm and would lead by example on the pitch and the training field.'

Highly rated Liverpool youngster David Thompson was signed for £2.5m. While not a direct replacement for McAllister, he would be tasked with providing some of the creativity that left the building along with the talismanic Scot. In a strange quirk, McAllister himself was key in the signing.

'I was due to sign a new contract at Liverpool because I'd activated it after making 25 appearances the season before,' Thompson explains. 'They didn't offer me as much as I thought I was going to get. I felt I'd done well the previous season and began to establish myself as a first-team player. They'd signed Nick Barmby as well for £8m and I assumed he was going to play on the right and he was an England international at the time. I assumed he had been signed to replace me. I had every confidence in fighting for my place as I thought I was a better player than Nick and I could offer a lot more to Liverpool. I just felt a bit disrespected and fed up. I rejected the contract and said to Gérard Houllier that if any clubs came in for me, I'd like them to notify me. The very next day they told me Coventry had put a bid in. I think it came about because Gary McAllister knew my situation and, because we'd been training together for a few weeks, he realised I wasn't a bad player and he recommended me to Gordon Strachan.'

Norwich's electric forward Craig Bellamy was the second big-money signing and he joined in a £6.5m deal. Cédric Roussel had finished the previous season fantastically, having formed a formidable partnership with the now departed Keane. For him, the change wasn't a positive one.

'I arrived at the training ground and Robbie asked to speak to me,' Roussel recalls. 'He said, "I'm off. I'm going to Inter Milan." I was so sad. Craig Bellamy was a fantastic player but I never got that same feeling that I did with Robbie. Bellamy was more selfish. With Robbie, we could play and it didn't matter who scored or who got the assists. With Craig, he was more selfish, he wanted the highlights, he was looking for his statistics.'

One big character who remained at the club was Carlton Palmer. His influence was greatly reduced, however, after a fall-out with Strachan.

'You lose your characters, you lose your best players, then you're going to have a problem,' Palmer says, assessing the issue facing the club at the start of the season. 'Gary McAllister was a leader, he was a character and a great player. You lose those types of players, then you are going to struggle. A manager has to understand that and to be able to deal with it. As a player you have to respect the manager and the other players in the team, I understand that. But if somebody is bringing something to the table, then you've got to work with them. If it's a good enough player, then you have to manage them. Ron Atkinson was able to do that with big players, your Paul McGraths, your Bryan Robsons and people like that. He used to call me in and put it on me and then on I went. Unfortunately, I had a fall-out with Strachan over something that I believed he went too far with. If that hadn't happened I would have been at Coventry for longer. It was sad how it ended. At the end of the day Carlton Palmer is Carlton Palmer and Gordon Strachan is Gordon Strachan. I've always had great respect for him and I always will do, he was a top-class player, top-class bloke and a top-class manager. But when you bring a character in you've got to be able to manage the character. It's difficult when you become a manager and you've got somebody like me. I liked to drink and I was a character but I also have always delivered on the pitch. Always. I think maybe Gordon was thinking about the young players coming through and he didn't really want me around those young players. My thing always was that if I went for a drink I would never take anyone with me. I never did. I never encouraged younger players to drink. You can ask Robbie Keane. He used to be in the hotel with me on a Friday night and I always used to have a bottle of wine on a Friday night and I never encouraged him to drink. He never had a drink. I played that way all through my career.'

Strachan too speaks of the detrimental impact of losing characters from the dressing room.

'We started to lose good men and, if you look at your career as a manager, you need good people,' he says. 'What went wrong at Coventry was recruitment. The recruitment was wrong. That was the downfall, absolutely. People might say that's not taking responsibility but I'm the one who signed them, so I'm taking every responsibility. That group that we had that you could trust with your life was suddenly dispersing.'

Regardless of the loss of such stellar characters, I approached 2000/01 with a smattering of excitement and confidence. Keane had been such a hit the previous year, perhaps Bellamy could be even better. Yes, McAllister was gone but we still had Hadji and Chippo, while Thompson looked a real talent. That confidence took a hefty dent on the opening day as Coventry fell to a 3-1 defeat at home to Middlesbrough. 'Boro's £2.5m summer signing Alen Bokšić absolutely ran City's defence ragged and bagged a brace. John Eustace scored for the Sky Blues from a Thompson cross, but the latter then marked his debut with a red card. He picked up two bookings, the second for a tired-looking tackle on Paul Ince.

'I hadn't really had a pre-season,' Thompson says. 'I'd trained for about five days but I was desperate to get amongst it. I thought I played really well for the first hour but then my fitness levels just dropped completely. I mistimed a tackle and then mistimed one in the corner with Paul. He used his experience and it was one I really should have avoided. I felt like I let the team down. That was immaturity from me. I should have asked to have been substituted before then.'

As for Bellamy, he looked lively, undoubtedly had pace but his debut fell well short of the impossibly high standards set by Keane's 12 months earlier. Let's not forget that Bellamy had been out for the previous year with a serious knee injury (the dreaded ACL) and some rustiness was perhaps to be expected. My abiding memory of the match was Bellamy hitting a shot from outside the box that trickled into Mark Schwarzer's gloves. We ended the 90 minutes with the jury still out on the new hitman. From new strikers to old ones, the match also saw the somewhat unsettling sight of Noel Whelan lining up in a Middlesbrough shirt. Whelan had made the £2m switch to Teesside in the summer after a five-year stay at Coventry.

'Coventry offered me a fantastic contract but I felt I needed a change, not just in career but in location,' Whelan explains. 'I needed to not have to deal with certain things anymore and have people talking about shop windows and this, that and the other. Even now, you get people mentioning that 25 years later, which is ridiculous. I went to Middlesbrough and I could live closer to my family in Leeds. I don't have one moment of regret from Coventry, even with everything off the field. It was a great dressing room, there wasn't a single person that nobody liked. Training was hard but fun. It was competitive at times. I didn't like losing even if it was a five-a-side or head tennis. I was that competitive and I might have put a few people out of action for a week or so but it was always a laugh afterwards. I just loved my time there.'

But from the doom and gloom quickly came a ray of light. The club had famously gone through the entire previous season without an away win, so of course they went and won not just their first away match of the new campaign, but their second as well. A pair of 2-1 wins, the first against Southampton and then Manchester City a few days later, meant a healthy six points out of nine. Bellamy also bagged a goal in each. Robbie who? Gordon Strachan had a typically Gordon Strachan suggestion for the club's upturn in fortunes on the road.

'In an interview [after the second away win] someone said to me that our away form was getting far better and I said, tongue in cheek, "Yeah, it's because we've changed the bus driver." But the bus driver got all upset! He wrote to the club complaining.'

Such flippant remarks were not uncommon from the gaffer.

'Gordon was interesting to deal with,' says Andy Turner. 'I've got a lot of time for him. I was just a young reporter at the time and it was my first experience of dealing with a manager. It could be quite intimidating at times. Sometimes you just couldn't get a straight answer. That was his character and I look back now and it's funny. I remember being at Elland Road and Gary Breen was injured. It was the post-match interview and I went through the questions about the game and then at the end got to injury news. I said something like, "How far away is Gary Breen?" Strachan, as quick as a flash, said, "He's 120 miles away down the motorway in Coventry." Then he just wouldn't answer the question! He'd come out with stuff like that. He tore a strip off me a few times, that was frightening. One time Huckerby turned around and said to me, "Now you know what we've been through!"'

Back to on-the-pitch matters and the Sky Blues went into the fourth match of the season, a home fixture with Newcastle, in the unusual position of knowing the winner would go top of the table. It was the Magpies who ran out 2-0 victors, which included a goal from City old boy Kevin Gallacher. It was here that Strachan made his offer to step aside. A 2-2 draw with Charlton followed, in which Bellamy netted his third in eight matches (an emphatically converted penalty) and John Aloisi bagged his fourth goal in a matter of days, having struck a midweek hat-trick in a 7-2 aggregate win over Preston in the League Cup. After the Charlton draw, *Match of the Day*'s Gerald Sinstadt commented in the post-match interview that Strachan's opposite number, Alan

Curbishley, was unsure whether to be happy or upset with a point, so how did Strachan feel? The Sky Blues boss replied, 'Scottish, determined and looking for a cup of tea.'

A win over Spurs followed, in which teen goalkeeper Chris Kirkland made his debut. A dreadful run was to follow, though, with just one point picked up from the next seven matches, a run that included some absolute shockers. A 2-1 loss to Bradford, the team that would finish the season rock bottom, 6-1 and 4-1 drubbings to Chelsea (in which Kirkland was sent off) and Liverpool (where McAllister well and truly pulled the strings), respectively, and a 1-0 home loss to newly promoted Ipswich left more than lingering doubts that this might be a tough season after all.

The Ipswich defeat was a particularly disappointing one; I can still recall the feeling of deflation as full-back Fabian Wilnis fired in a late winner for the visitors. Perhaps the worst of that run, though, was a 3-0 defeat at Highfield Road to West Ham. In fairness, this West Ham team was pretty tasty, you only have to look at the goalscorers that day to realise that (Di Canio, Lampard and Cole), but this felt like a watershed defeat. This was the angriest I can recall Highfield Road being during a match. There seemed real vitriol aimed at the players, the coaching staff and the board. The change in atmosphere didn't go unnoticed.

'It was horrible,' Bryan Richardson remembers of fans calling for Strachan to be sacked. 'Sometimes when you have that sort of atmosphere it makes you more determined to stick with what you think is right. The nastiness of some upset Gordon, it upset me and you put a brave face on it because you have to. People should have realised that Gordon came in as a player and single-handedly kept us up. He made the likes of Keane and Dion. A lot of these players were on good contracts, playing well in the Premier League because of Gordon. It was very short-sighted of people to want to sack Gordon.'

An issue that dogged the club that season was that Coventry's backline was far too often patched together with square pegs forced into round holes. In goal, Magnus Hedman and Kirkland switched in and out regularly due to a mix of injury and form – throughout the league season Hedman started 15 times with Kirkland playing in the remaining 23 matches. Full-back was where the real uncertainty was though. With Froggatt on the sidelines for the entire campaign and David Burrows having left for Birmingham City in the summer, right-footers Barry Quinn and Marc Edworthy often filled in at left-back. Meanwhile, over on the other side there was the use of centre-half Gary Breen. Richard Shaw missed 14 of the 38 matches, while Paul Williams featured in 30. That still left a fair chunk of matches without at least one of the club's recognised first-choice defensive pairing. In such instances, Breen usually came in at his natural position, with two from Edworthy, Quinn and Marcus Hall at full-back. To a man, these are all solid players, but the lack of a rock-solid back five seemed to create problems. This poor run of form saw City drop into the relegation zone and Strachan sought to address matters by bringing in midfielder Lee Carsley in a £2.5m deal from Blackburn. One of Carsley's first matches came against Leicester. Fellow new boy Bellamy put in one of his best performances in a Coventry shirt and scored the winner in a 1-0 to kick-start a mini revival. Just one defeat in the next six followed, including a late win against Everton, courtesy of a Breen goal.

But the topsy-turvy form continued – early 2001 saw four defeats in a row, including a painful 3-1 loss to Everton at Highfield Road. It was a defeat that left Strachan in desperately low spirits.

'We got beat at Everton that season and Archie Knox was a coach there and he's a friend, so he came over to the house,' Strachan explains. 'The next morning I woke up and people were still in the house and I went on a walk and I ended up walking to Wellesbourne with my good shoes on! Lesley, my wife, had to come and get me. I just walked and kept walking because I didn't want to talk to anybody.'

'We lost at home to Everton and Gordon was very down,' Richardson adds. 'We shouldn't have lost that game but did. I told Gordon I'd call into his house on the way home for a chat. I called in and we had a chat in his kitchen and he was down, very down. I told him he was a fine manager, he was everything that we needed and he mustn't doubt himself. I told him the players respected him and it was up to him now to pull himself together and be the leader that the club needed.'

Strachan's mood won't have been lifted by the defeats to Leeds and Arsenal that followed. Both were 1-0 losses, with Robbie Keane coming back to haunt his former employers with the only goal at Elland Road. These defeats left City five points from safety at the start of February. Things were bleak and the club's never-ending injury list did little to improve matters.

Team	P	GD	Pts
17. Middlesbrough	26	-3	26
18. Manchester City	26	-13	23
19. Coventry	26	-22	21
20. Bradford	25	-30	16

'I was injured quite a lot that season and I played with injuries,' says David Thompson. 'I almost ruptured my ligaments in my left leg on a traffic cone at the training ground before a game and Gordon said as long as I could take the corners and free kicks then I would play. It was against Charlton at home [on 24 February] and I had a 50-50 with Andy Todd and did my ankle again. I had a bit of a stinker. I couldn't run with the ankle and I shouldn't have been out there. We went in at half-time and before I could say anything he singled me out and said, "Thommo, what's going on out there, you're having a shocker, every pass is a stinker." I was thinking he'd only played me to take the set pieces and here he was highlighting me in front of everyone!'

Thompson speaks today with little regret that he played through the pain barrier, but is honest in saying that had there been other options he may have been able to nurse himself back to full fitness.

'If we'd had a little bit more quality in the squad, then I wouldn't have felt the pressure that I would be letting the lads down if I didn't play,' he says. 'I was frustrated. I felt if I was fully fit I could have contributed and we could have stayed up.'

The other major addition to the squad that season also continued to struggle. Bellamy had shown glimpses of his potential but was clearly still a way off from 100 per cent after his injury the previous year and had fallen well short of the standard set by Keane. Many of us looking on from the outside also wondered about the Welshman's character and how he slotted into the squad.

'They doubled their money on Keane but signing Bellamy as his replacement, more as a character than anything else, that was the wrong decision,' reckons Rob Gurney. 'I think that did affect the dressing room quite adversely. He was, from my recollections, the definition of Billy Big Time. He thought he was all that. I think he was the wrong type of character. Bellamy didn't have many allies in the dressing room. At another club, if you had loads of big egos, you can sustain another player with a big ego. But I'd always regarded City as a club where team spirit was so important. I think Bellamy was too divisive a character.'

I must say, prior to starting work on this book, I had heard rumblings of Bellamy being a disruptive influence in the camp. During the process of interviewing former players and managers, however, not a single one of the squad from that time had anything negative to say about him. Instead, it was a story of him being the right player at the wrong time.

'Craig was a good lad,' says Thompson. 'He had a lot of

confidence but he also had a lot of ability. He hated losing. He was a bit spiky in the dressing room and he upset a few people because he was so honest. Maybe he didn't structure his words in the right way. A lot of players found him quite cutting. I loved him in the dressing room. He was always first in the training ground and last out. His dedication to the game was second to none. Craig was always out practising his shooting. Balls would be going here, there and everywhere and some lads were thinking, "Bloody hell, how much have we paid for this lad?" But you could see his quality. You could see his work rate and his desire to win.'

'If Bellamy and Thompson had come in two years earlier they would have loved it,' says Richard Shaw. 'They were wonderful footballers. They were in the right team at the wrong time. We were just struggling and didn't have the characters to see games through. We struggled with squad depth. We brought in Runar Normann and Zungia. They were great lads but they weren't another Hadji and Chippo. You're only as good as your No.9. We'd gone from Dion Dublin to I don't know what. Cédric did as best as he could and had some good games alongside Robbie. Craig didn't have much support and probably needed a big man around him because he was so quick. John Aloisi was a good player but needed help up there. It was difficult.'

Thompson had also found the move a tricky transition and admits that, while he loved his time at Coventry and didn't regret the switch from Liverpool, it was a different ball game at Highfield Road in comparison with Anfield.

'I went from dominating games at Liverpool with 70 per cent possession and I found it difficult at Coventry because we didn't have the ball as much,' he says. 'I was having to work harder off the ball and then, when we did get the ball, I was expected to assume the role of creator, whereas at Liverpool you can be very patient. You can move the ball around, you don't have to take risks with the ball because things will open up eventually because you're dominating possession. At Coventry I felt I was always trying to force things and be extra creative because there weren't many of us in that team who could be.'

It wasn't just the new signings that struggled; stars from the previous season failed to hit their stride, including both Moroccans.

'Chippo the previous season was fantastic but he got tapped up by an agent,' suggests Bryan Richardson. 'Gordon was told that Bobby Robson wanted Chippo at Newcastle. He was told if we didn't give him £10,000 a week, then he would go to Newcastle. Gordon said, "Okay, I'll ring Bobby now and ask him." Gordon did ring Bobby and Bobby said he thought Chippo was one hell of a player but he wasn't for them because they had X, Y and Z in midfield and they didn't need him. That unsettled Chippo. That year he wasn't the player that he was.'

Another problem that dogged the season was a tendency to concede late goals. Strachan's teams had previously been built around fitness and often came on strong in the latter part of matches and the final third of the season. This time points were being dropped too often from goals in the final ten minutes of matches. Just under a quarter of the total league goals conceded by City this season came in the final ten minutes (accounting for 15 out of 63 goals). Without these late goals, the Sky Blues would have amassed an extra 15 points during the season. The fitness regime hadn't changed, so perhaps this was another issue caused by the loss of big characters on and off the pitch.

'I remember Gordon thinking we lacked a bit of fitness because we conceded so many late goals,' says Thompson. 'I don't think it was a lack of fitness because we trained so hard. We worked hard in games but I think we just lacked a little bit of quality and confidence. When you're not confident, if it's 1-1 with 20 minutes to go, you start thinking, "Oh god, we've had chances to win this, now let's hang on for a draw." What happens then is you retreat, concede ground and you concede a goal late on. That's deflating and it became a regular occurrence for us.'

'When you're in a battle you have to have a special kind of character,' Magnus Hedman adds. 'You have to have mentally strong people. When we went through that tough spell in the relegation season you could notice that people got injured easier. You could see some players could play great at home but were completely different away from home. That is a mental thing. Conceding late goals is definitely a mental thing. Feeling tired is mental. It depends how much you let that get to you. The longer a game goes, the more nervous you will get if you're thinking, "Oh, we can't lose this, we can't lose this." If you think that way you will stop yourself from performing 100 per cent.'

Thompson was adamant that the spate of late goals was not a fitness issue and took his case to the gaffer.

'I had an argument with Gordon one time at the training ground,' he says. 'We were both convinced that we were right. I said we were doing too much during the week. I said it wasn't fitness that we were lacking, it was fatigue that was setting in in the last 20 minutes of games. All of the boys were honest lads, we all wanted to win and were doing our best. We didn't have any slackers in the team. Even Hadji, who was a flair player, used to work his balls off. We'd had this disagreement on the training ground and then about a week later the gaffer named the team for a game and I wasn't in it. I was confused, I hadn't been playing badly and the lads were always trying to get me on the ball because they knew I could do something. Bellamy said, "Gaffer, you've made a mistake there because Thommo's not in the team." Strachan has ignored him and Craig's gone again, "Gaffer, you've made a mistake, Thommo's not in the team." My head had gone and I walked off the training pitch and I can hear the gaffer saying, "Shut up, Craig, just fucking shut up, Craig.'"

Away from the camp, fans were understandably unhappy with how the season was panning out. Rob Gurney hosted the Friday night phone-in on BBC Coventry and Warwickshire and one particular caller landed the broadcaster in hot water with the under-pressure Strachan.

'One of my regrets is how things between us panned out,' Gurney says of his relationship with Strachan. 'For the first few seasons, he was excellent to deal with. I got on very well with him. Then in the relegation season I sensed a change. As the results got worse, I was getting it from all sides. The fans thought I was giving the club too easy a ride, certainly by the turn of 2001 onwards. We fell out over something on the phone-in about that Strachan wouldn't get the sack because him and the chairman go away on holiday together. That was never me who said that, it was a caller. I think because I didn't knock that down as much as they wanted me to knock that down, and relegation was looming, that's why it came to a head and Gordon didn't directly speak to me for five months. I could go to press conferences but I couldn't ask any questions. Then, as quickly as it started it finished and one day he said I could lead off with the questions. But things were never the same again. You try to build a relationship but when things get difficult you have to be able to ask the difficult questions. Garry Pendrey pretty much physically pinned me to the wall in the dressing room at the training ground and was bellowing in my ear about what I had said. I tried to repair things a little bit over the years but it fell on deaf ears. A few years ago when he was doing ITV punditry I would see him at games and he would look through me. It's sad that things panned out like that but he's a very strong character.'

Poor performances on the pitch, late goals flying in, a breakdown in communication between boss and media – things were about as bad as they could get. Relegation was looking a certainty. With time running out, the Sky Blues needed a saviour. The man they looked to was Wimbledon striker John Hartson. Unfortunately, the fiery Welshman's signing dragged on for an absolute eternity. Rumours circulated that Cédric Roussel would need to be sold before the move for Hartson could be funded, but all who I've spoken to have claimed that instead it was purely a medical issue that slowed down the deal.

'That year I failed a couple of big medicals before the Coventry deal,' says Hartson. 'I'd failed a medical at Spurs for a £7m transfer. I also failed one at Charlton for £5.5m. Something was showing up on the scans on my knee. They were saying my knee wouldn't hold up to rigorous training every day. Gordon Strachan called me one day while I was on the golf course and asked if I would want to come to Coventry and I told him absolutely. They had a great bunch of players there. I told him I'd love to go to Coventry. Coventry tried to thrash a deal out with Wimbledon and my knee was absolutely fine, it was just something showing up on the scan. I was training absolutely fine. Gordon was on the phone most nights asking what was happening and I would say I didn't know and he needed to ring the club and speak to the chairman because we needed to get it done. It was frustrating because we could have got that deal done earlier.'

Whether his move was key in financing the Hartson transfer or not, Roussel was on his way out. A transfer to Wimbledon broke down before Wolves came in and signed the Belgian.

'Coventry was the best time I had in my career,' Roussel says. 'I will always love Coventry. I knew Coventry needed money, that's why I left. Gordon said he wanted to keep me but they needed the money. It was difficult to tell my family I was leaving Coventry. I had to put it into my mind that I was going. I had met a girlfriend and I had a child and when I understood that I had to go I knew that I wanted to stay in Leamington, that was my home. It would have been too difficult to move to London and settle again. Going to Wolves meant I was leaving but not completely. We played against Coventry [the following season] at Highfield Road and the fans stood up and started to chant my name. I was crying. When I went out, I instinctively went to the Coventry bench and Gordon had to tell me I was on the wrong side! Something broke when I left Coventry, I was upset to leave.'

After weeks of wranglings, the Hartson deal finally went through. He came in for £700,000 up front, with further payments based on appearances. Barry Quinn was one of many who was impressed by the new signing right off the bat.

'Hartson was a good guy, proper old school,' says Quinn. 'He hated the running. Monday morning after a game you'd come in and hit the ground running with training and be running and he'd be like, "Nah, I can't do this!" I'll tell you what though, he knew where the net was. Put the ball in that 18-yard box and he'd score. As a full-back, he was a great out ball. If you could get it to him, his protection of the ball was brilliant. If you were under pressure and could pick out the right ball to him, then nine times out of ten he would hold on to that ball and get you up the park. His ball retention was brilliant. Over five or ten yards he was so sharp. Get the ball to him in the box and he was so quick on to it. We didn't have another player like him that season. At the end of that season, we had these pressurised games and we needed someone like him who could dominate a centre-half in these pressure games when it was a battle. You'd have Hartson for that all day.'

Hartson knew the enigmatic Bellamy from the Wales international set-up and his arrival seemed to light a spark with the £6.5m signing.

'I already knew Craig from playing for Wales and they partnered us up top, with John Eustace in the middle of the park; he was a very good, very combative player,' says Hartson. 'Gordon basically built the team around me. He put me down the middle and told everyone to get the ball to me so I could hold it up and ruffle a few feathers along the way. It just worked, for some reason it just clicked. We had some really good wins. I started to enjoy my football again. Gordon always felt that if you were relaxed and you enjoyed the environment you were in then that would bring out the best in players. I absolutely loved it there.'

Hartson made his debut in a 1-1 draw with West Ham, having a goal dubiously ruled out. His second appearance came at home to Charlton and both he and Bellamy found the net in a 2-2 draw. A point was a missed opportunity and not enough to raise real survival hopes, but did at least indicate that we finally had a strike force. Hartson is acutely aware that his arrival allowed Bellamy to flourish for the final handful of matches of the season.

'We had Darren Grewcock, the fitness coach, and Craig would spend hours with him in the gym at Coventry working on his sprints,' he says. 'I've never seen a harder worker than Craig Bellamy in terms of what he does outside of the games and what he does to work on his body, fitness and his speed. He would spend hours in the gym after everybody had gone home. He had a tough time that season and I think Craig himself puts a lot of his form at the end of the season down to big John arriving. He knew that big John, myself, would partner up with him and we had done that for Wales. It took a bit of pressure off him in terms of he wasn't the only one everyone was expecting something from. He could just relax and go play his football. Craig let me take all of the fouls. People could bash me around and, if the ball bounced out to the right, Craig could get on the ball and make things happen for us. I could take that pressure off him and I feel that I did that for a while. It gave Craig that freedom. Craig can divide opinion but I like Craig. I knew him well and had come through with him at Wales, so I knew how to be with Craig and he was always fine with me.'

Back-to-back wins over Derby and Leicester, with Hartson on the scoresheet in both, suddenly gave fans some hope that the greatest of great escapes could be on. Following the 3-1 victory at Filbert Street, Coventry remained in the drop zone but were only two points behind Middlesbrough, albeit with a vastly inferior goal difference, and five away from Derby. It would be tough, but surviving is what Coventry did, right? A 4-2 loss at Old Trafford was a setback and again late goals were the problem, with two in the last ten minutes giving United the win.

'In the second half I couldn't believe it because we were holding out for a point when Ryan Giggs, who I had never seen score a goal with his head before, goes and scores a header from the edge of the box,' recalls Hartson. 'It was freakish. I'd played with Ryan for ten years for Wales and I knew he had a great leap and was a great player but to score that header showed that it just wasn't our day. It was Keane, Scholes, Giggs, Yorke, all of these guys were right on top of us towards the end and they were pushing and pushing. We just couldn't hold out. We'd played so well. I think we took some confidence from it, though, to know that we could go to Old Trafford and score twice and give them a game.'

The roller-coaster final third of the season continued as a Hartson goal was the difference in a 1-0 win over Sunderland. That left the Sky Blues still two points behind Middlesbrough and five from Derby but now there were only four matches left to play. Ipswich, who had dealt a body blow early in the season in a 1-0 defeat, were up next. Unfortunately, history repeated itself as the Tractor Boys notched a 2-0 win at Portman Road. A 2-0 home defeat to Liverpool came next and by this point all hope was pretty much gone. There was the unenviable task of having to go to Villa Park in the penultimate match of the season and needing a win.

Team	P	GD	Pts
16. Middlesbrough	36	-1	38
17. Derby	36	-23	38
18. Manchester City	36	-22	34
19. Coventry	36	-26	33

With two matches to play City had now slipped behind Manchester City into 19th. The gap to safety was now five points. Maximum points were needed and the hope that either Derby or Middlesbrough would lose both of their remaining matches. The memory of previous brushes with the drop left fans and players alike with the faintest of hopes that it could happen again.

'We'd had the escape at Tottenham before so we knew we could get out of it but we knew it was creeping up on us,' admits Marcus Hall. 'We went to the Forest of Arden on the morning of the game to change things up and give us a different bit of scenery. I remember sitting and thinking, "God, this game is massive." We knew it would be a massive atmosphere and they would definitely want to send us down.'

Incredibly, two Hadji goals put the Sky Blues 2-0 up. The greatest escape was back on. Alas, it wasn't to last. An injury to the much-maligned Paul Telfer forced a reshuffle on 38 minutes, with Marc Edworthy coming on. The loss of the utility man seemed to see the game plan fly out of the window.

'The Telfer injury rocked us,' Hall admits. 'We just collapsed. I don't think it was through our mentality. We had gone two up and I think Villa just stepped up their game.'

From two up at the interval, the second half was a disaster. Darius Vassell pulled one back just after the hour mark and then yet again those late goals proved decisive. Juan Pablo Ángel levelled on 81 minutes before Paul Merson curled in a long-range effort with just four minutes to play. As it turned out, even a win wouldn't have been enough as Derby went and pulled off a shock win against Manchester United to guarantee their safety, while Middlesbrough earned a 1-1 draw with bottom-of-the-table Bradford. The game was up. After 34 years in the top flight, Coventry had been relegated.

'It was a devastating day,' says Hall. 'For me, being from Coventry, I felt that responsibility that I was in the team that went down after the club had been up for so many years. I was living in Coventry and I was wondering how I was ever going to get over it and how was I going to be able to look people in the eye in the street. A lot of players lived maybe in Leamington but they didn't live in Coventry and do a school run in Coventry. I was also getting married that summer and my wife said to me, "Is our wedding going to be ruined now because you're going to be in a mood for the whole summer?" At the time I thought it was the worst thing that could have possibly happened to me. It was horrible. It was something we didn't really ever recover from.'

It was a feeling of despair but also frustration that the Hartson deal couldn't have been done even a few weeks sooner.

'Gordon always said if he could have got me sooner things would have been different,' says Hartson. 'I couldn't believe a team like that could get relegated. There were good players in that dressing room. If I'd had the full season there it could have been a lot different, I could have got the goals that would have kept us up. We'll never know but I did really hit the ground running when I got there. I enjoyed the camaraderie that the club had. It was a good dressing room. Chris Kirkland went on to Liverpool, Bellamy to Newcastle, Hadji to Villa, Telfer to Celtic, we had really good players. The boys just needed something extra to give them a boost and some momentum and that was nearly me. It was nearly enough.'

There was still one match to play out to conclude the season. In perhaps the most depressing Premier League fixture of all time, two already-relegated teams met on the final day as Bradford visited Highfield Road for a typically uninspiring 0-0 draw.

'There was so much disappointment that day,' Barry Quinn recalls. 'We didn't play well. It's a hard game to play in. It's not about motivating yourself but it was a very strange game to end the season on.'

With the season finally over, attention switched to what many, myself included, thought would be a triumphant one-year stay in the second tier. Many fans had wanted Strachan out during the season but he retained the support of both the board and his playing squad and would lead the club into the new season. On the playing side, changes were inevitable. Ultimately, while the signing of Hartson came too late to save the club, it was a cut-price deal that provided some financial solace.

'Coventry did well because the deal was done that they would pay the fee over a certain amount of time, with payments for playing a certain amount of times,' Gordon Strachan recalls. 'It was £700,000 with three-point-something million to follow. Well, we only had to pay £700,000 because he was sold that summer. Whoever did that deal at Wimbledon didn't do their sums right and it wasn't in the proviso what would happen if he was sold, so we only paid the initial payment.'

'John Hartson was a great deal for us,' Bryan Richardson adds. 'We tried and tried to get John weeks earlier. I kept going at Wimbledon and in the end we did a deal. That summer we were in Ireland for pre-season and the Celtic chairman Dermot Desmond and Martin O'Neill wanted big John. There was a decorator in Dermot's house in London and he heard him on the telephone talking to Martin saying they wanted to sign big John and they were sure he'd come because he didn't want to play in the Championship. The decorator was a Coventry fan and he told me the story. So when I was in Dublin on pre-season and Dermot said he'd like to meet, I knew what it was about. He said he'd like to buy John Hartson, and I said, "Yes, I gathered so." He asked how much I wanted for him and I said £8m. He said, "What! How much did you pay for him?" I told him that was no concern of his. In the end we agreed £6m plus £1m depending on games. I don't know if Dermot ever found out what we had paid for him.'

For Hartson, his decision to leave was made easier when he saw others heading for the exit, as Bellamy moved to Newcastle and Hadji followed Dublin and Boateng to Villa.

'I can honestly say if Coventry had kept Bellamy and Hadji that summer, we would have had a great chance of getting back up,' Hartson says. 'I got on really well with Bryan Richardson but I think the Ricoh Arena was well in sight at the time and I think he decided to make £16m overnight by selling me, Bellamy and Hadji. I don't want to speak poorly of Bryan, but Coventry have never been back up. Gordon tried everything to keep me, he really did. He offered me the captaincy, he offered me a better role within the club where I could do a bit of coaching as well in a similar way to what he did with Howard Wilkinson at Leeds. He said, "John, on the back of how we finished last season you have to come back." I'd had this offer from Celtic and an offer from Middlesbrough, and when I saw Craig and Hadji leaving I thought it was a bit of a lack of ambition. I couldn't stay when they'd just sold two of our best players. If we had any chance of coming back up we had to all stick together as a team and do it. From my heart I believe if we had been a bit more patient then we would have had a great chance of coming back up because we had a phenomenal group of players. We would have taken that league by storm. Not long into that season Gordon got the sack and it all unravelled. That was such a shame.'

Another striker on his way out was John Aloisi. The Australian had struggled with injury throughout his time at the club and there were doubts over whether he could sustain the 46-match season that was on the way.

'I wanted to stay after relegation and I spoke to Strachan

about it,' he says. 'I could understand his side, I had been in and out of the side because of injury. I felt that, because I had played in the Championship, I could do really well in the Championship and help the team get promoted. He said they wanted to change things up and bring in new faces. He explained that because of the injuries that I'd had it would be a risk to have me as the number-one striker. I completely understood. I moved to La Liga and maybe that helped me because it was one game a week instead of three. I was disappointed to not get to stay at Coventry but maybe it was the best thing for me to move abroad.'

After a disappointing start to 2001/02, Strachan was sacked just a few matches into the season. He took with him a relegation on his CV that undoubtedly tarnishes his Coventry legacy, despite having been at the helm for some of the most exciting football the club had ever seen.

'It would be great if people appreciated that for five or six seasons we did well,' he says. 'People will say I got the sack but I lasted six years there working very hard. The problem was that we went above what was realistic for us and we spent too much money. I was a young manager and left the finances to everybody else.'

'He will always be the manager that took Coventry down after 34 years,' Andy Turner says. 'He will always carry the can for that. But, if you're a rational Coventry City fan you can look back with fondness. He made two or three different teams, we had the Huckerby, Dublin, Whelan era, the Moroccans, Keane, McAllister, the Swedish internationals, we were attracting internationals and players who played at World Cups.'

'Any manager that takes a club down is going to be frowned upon, but look at his body of work there and the players that he worked with and what he did for them,' Huckerby adds. 'Look at the players that he had to sell – for me that's the biggest thing. If you have a two-year period where you're having to sell Dion Dublin, George Boateng, Darren Huckerby, Robbie Keane, Noel Whelan, I don't care who the team is, if you sell five of your best players in a two-year period, you're going to get relegated. If Gordon had been allowed to keep the players that he wanted to it would have been different.'

Coventry's roller-coaster Premier League tenure was over. The club had been early leaders of the first Premier League, upset the big boys with wins over Arsenal, Manchester United, Liverpool and Chelsea and survived when the odds were stacked against us. In that time we had enjoyed the arrival of internationals from all over the world, celebrated sublime goals and saluted genuine club legends. There aren't any trophies to show for those nine seasons and they ended with our exit into the second tier. Fingers can, and should, be pointed in numerous directions for the shambles that followed: the financial mismanagement, the farce of our departure from Highfield Road and the stadium woes that have dogged us ever since. But as I look back on the football from those years, I do so with a huge amount of pride and enjoyment. These were the years that I grew up on as a Coventry fan, years during which we mixed it with the big boys and, sometimes, came out on top. Let's hope one day for a return to the top flight and another decade-spanning stint at the top table, ushering in a time when we can all once again sing, 'While the sky is blue, we'll never lose.'